Praise for the series:

Passionate, obsessive, and smart—*Nylon*

Religious tracts for the rock'n'roll faithful—*Boldtype*

Each volume has a distinct, almost militantly personal take on a beloved long-player . . . the books that have resulted are like the albums themselves—filled with moments of shimmering beauty, forgivable flaws, and stubborn eccentricity—*Tracks Magazine*

At their best, these books make rich, thought-provoking arguments for the song collections at hand—*The Philadelphia Inquirer*

Praise for individual books in the series:

Dusty in Memphis

Warren Zanes . . . is so in love with Dusty Springfield's great 1969 adventure in tortured Dixie soul that he's willing to jump off the deep end in writing about it—*Rolling Stone*

A heartfelt dive into the world of 60s R&B . . . dazzling—*Pop Culture Press*

A long, scholarly, and convincing piece of nonfiction analyzing the myth of the American South—Nick Hornby, *The Believer*

Forever Changes

Hultkrans obsesses brilliantly on the rock legends' seminal disc—*Vanity Fair*

Exemplary . . . a wonderful piece of writing—*Pop Culture Press*

Great . . . the writing and approach matches the enduring complexity of its subject—Jon Savage, *Word*

The Kinks Are The Village Green Preservation Society

This is the sort of focus that may make you want to buy a copy, or dig out your old one—*The Guardian*

This detailed tome leads the reader through the often fraught construction of what is now regarded as Davies's masterpiece—and, like the best books of its ilk, it makes the reader want to either reinvestigate the album or hear it for the first time—*Blender Magazine*

Fascinating and superbly researched . . . a book that every Kinks fan will love—*Record Collector*

Meat Is Murder

Full of mordant wit and real heartache. A dead-on depiction of what it feels like when pop music articulates your pain with an elegance you could never hope to muster. 'Meat is Murder' does a brilliant job of capturing how, in a world that doesn't care, listening to your favorite album can save your life—*The Philadelphia Inquirer*

Like his exquisite LPs, Pernice's perceptive, poetic ear for unpicking the workings of troubled inner lives is exceptional—*Uncut*

A slim, confessional novella equal to anything written by Nick Hornby—*Bandoppler*

One can accept, reluctantly, Pernice's apparently inexhaustible ability to knock out brilliant three-minute pop songs. But now it turns out that he can write fiction too, and so envy and bitterness become unavoidable—Nick Hornby, *The Believer*

The Piper at the Gates of Dawn

John Cavanagh combines interviews with early associates of Pink Floyd and recording-studio nitty-gritty to vividly capture the first and last flush of Syd Barrett's psychedelic genius on the Floyd's '67 debut—*Rolling Stone*

Digs impressively deep . . . a must-have for Syd-era Floyd fans—*Record Collector*

Harvest

Successfully sets the album both in its time and within the artist's canon—*Record Collector*

Live at the Apollo

Also available in this series

Forthcoming in this series

Live at the Apollo

Douglas Wolk

continuum
NEW YORK · LONDON

2004

The Continuum International Publishing Group Inc
15 E 26 Street, New York, NY 10010

The Continuum International Publishing Group Ltd
The Tower Building, 11 York Road, London SE1 7NX

www.continuumbooks.com

Copyright © 2004 by Douglas Wolk

Printed in the United States of America

Library of Congress Cataloging-in-Publication Data

Wolk, Douglas.
Live at the Apollo / Douglas Wolk.
p. cm. — (33 1/3)
Includes bibliographical references and index.
ISBN 0-8264-1572-5 (pbk. : alk. paper)
1. Brown, James, 1928- Apollo Theater presents,
in person, the James Brown show. 2. Apollo Theathre
(New York, N.Y.) I. Title. II. Series.
ML420.B818W65 2004
782.421644'092—dc22
2004006573

"JAMES BROWN (THANKS)"

Thanks to Dr. David Barker for inviting me to do this project, to Lisa Gidley for putting up with it, and to Harry Weinger, Hal Neely, Chuck Seitz and John Tanner for their valuable assistance. Extra special thanks to Alan Leeds for information and assistance way above and beyond the call of any imaginable duty.

TODD GITLIN, ON THE WEEK OF OCTOBER 24, 1962, IN HIS BOOK *THE SIXTIES*

"Time was deformed, everyday life suddenly dwarfed and illuminated, as if by the glare of an explosion that had not yet taken place."

DIONYSUS LIVE AT THE APOLLO

In the fall of 1962, the Apollo Theater's stage area appeared to its audience as a box, twice as wide as it was tall. The worn-down wooden planks of the stage floor were perpendicular to the audience. Originally a burlesque house, Hurtig & Seamon's Music Hall, the Apollo had "turned black" in 1934, as risqué stage shows fell to a city crackdown and vaudeville lost the last of its territory to the talkies. Located "in the heart of friendly Harlem," as its ads said, at 125th Street off Eighth Avenue in Manhattan, it booked star acts to play for a solid week, in front of the toughest and most devoted crowds they'd ever face. By the early '60s, the Apollo was well established as the crown jewel of the "chitlin circuit"—the network of small and large halls, mostly in the South and on the East Coast, where black artists would play to black audiences, touring as hard as they could bear.

Standing on the stage of the Apollo at a sold-out show on the night of October 24, 1962, screaming, James Brown would have looked out and seen 1500 people screaming back at him in the audience, split between the floor and the balconies. The walls behind them were a dark crimson; the balconies were decorated with the laurel wreaths that are the emblem of Apollo the god, recalling Daphne, who became a laurel tree to escape his lust. Most of the audience thought there was a good chance they'd be dead within the week.

That night, on stage at the Apollo, James Brown made a new kind of pop record, based on the force of a single, superhuman will, and built around performance itself, even more than performances of particular songs. *Live at the Apollo* is one of the most *charged* albums ever made—electrical arcs fly between Brown and his terrified, ecstatic, howling audience.

Brown has built the structures of the album around himself, so that he can break free of them. Every word and note that *doesn't* come from him, beginning with the opening incantation and ending with the chorus that ends the record, is ritualized, precise, formally scripted; his own performance is unrestricted and overwhelming, an explosion about to take place at the intersection of lust and terror. The moment of sexual abandonment (and erotic abandon) was the subject of all of James Brown's great songs in those days. He sings as if his lover leaving him would be the end of the world, which is also a way of singing about the end of the world. The song ceases to be the song, and becomes James Brown. "Supernatural sounds emanate from him," as Friedrich Nietzsche wrote about man under the charm of the Dionysian. "He is no longer an artist; he has become a work of art."

It cost two dollars to get into the Apollo, and you could stay all day if you wanted to.

WHAT MIKHAIL POLONIK, THE SOVIET PRESS OFFICER AT THE UNITED NATIONS, TOLD AN AMERICAN OFFICIAL THE EVENING BEFORE THE EVENTS RELATED IN THIS BOOK

"This could well be our last conversation. New York will be blown up tomorrow by Soviet nuclear weapons."

THE ALBUM

Live at the Apollo doesn't say "Live at the Apollo" any-where on its front cover. The cover painting, by Dan Quest, is an indistinct, chunky watercolor of a crowd clustering around a marquee that looks a little like the Apollo's, framed by a white border; the only other sharp lines belong to something that's presumably a car pass-ing by the front. The type on the marquee says "The Apollo Theatre (*sic*) Presents - In Person! The James Brown ***Show***." The marquee's side panel adds "James Brown" and, below that, "Voted No. 1 R&B Star of 1962." The back cover explains that the vote came from a national poll of disc jockeys, although which national poll has never been clear.

On the original front cover, a King Records logo bulges out of the top right-hand corner of the painting. "Vivid Sound," declares a banner within the car shape down at the bottom—a tag-line that King put on many of its LPs in 1963 and 1964. ("That was just advertising," King's former chief engineer Chuck Seitz says. "Matter of fact, we were doing a lot of stuff with primitive equipment. Our main console was handmade.") The back cover's banner type reads "James Brown 'Live' at the Apollo," which is the title that caught on.

The title of the album has never quite stabilized, actually. When the Solid Smoke label reissued it in

1980, it was retitled *Live and Lowdown at the Apollo, Vol. 1*. (The Solid Smoke version is a real oddity, if you can track a copy down: unlike most stereo copies, which let the vocals and instruments overlap, it was mixed with the vocals all the way on one side and the instrumental parts all the way on the other. The company also released a DJ edition, which keeps "Lost Someone" in one piece on side 2, and displaces the long medley to the first side.) And where did that "lowdown" come from? Possibly from Marva Whitney's JB-produced 1969 album, *Live and Lowdown at the Apollo*. The Polydor CD that came out in 1990 is *James Brown Live at the Apollo, 1962*, to distinguish it from his three later *Apollo* albums. At least that's what it says on the spine—the disc itself is labeled as *The Apollo Theater Presents, In Person, The James Brown Show*. The 2004 edition is *James Brown Live at the Apollo (1962)*. For the purposes of this book, it's *Live at the Apollo* or LATA, but call it what you like.

HOW IT HAPPENED

In 1962, you could've gathered from James Brown's record sales that he was a reasonably successful R&B act—no Ray Charles or Jackie Wilson, certainly, but a solid, dependable singles artist, along the lines of, say, Bobby Bland. Where Brown really shone, though, was in performance. Constantly on the road and a scenery-chewing showman, he'd built up a huge following as a live act; for a few years, he'd been traveling with a full band and a supporting revue.

Brown got the notion in the fall of 1962 that a re-cording of his live show, along the lines of Ray Charles's 1959 LP *In Person*, would be a good idea. King Records president Syd Nathan, in one of a string of legendarily awful judgment calls that his business miraculously sur-vived, thought it was a terrible idea, and declared that nobody would ever buy it; he refused to fund a re-cording. King wasn't one of those big East Coast labels with a big promotional budget, it was an independent operation based in Cincinnati. It was in the business of putting out hit singles, and as far as Nathan was con-cerned the only reason anybody bought R&B albums was to get the singles, which of course wouldn't appear on a live album.

So Brown made his own arrangements to turn his show into a record. He spent $5700 recording the al-bum; instead of going for the usual deal with the Apollo where he would be paid a percentage of the door after expenses, he rented out the theater, and arranged for its employees to wear uniforms for his weeklong engage-ment there—the ushers wore tuxedos. The James Brown Revue opened at the Apollo on Friday, October 19, and ran through the following Thursday, October 25.

GETTING READY

On the night of October 22, President Kennedy had made a televised appearance announcing a U.S. naval blockade of Cuba, which began at 10 AM on the 24th: the Atlantic Fleet was told to shoot, if necessary, at Russian cargo ships bound for Cuba. Defense Secretary Robert McNamara had predicted on the evening of the 23rd that some sort of "challenge" might well happen within 24 hours. American stores, that week, were full of panic buyers, stockpiling food and supplies, but also buying appliances: they were not ready to have their lives end without a dishwasher or a television.

WHAT THEY WERE STOCKING UP ON IN THE RECORD STORES

According to the local Top 40 station WMCA, the best-selling record in New York City stores the week of October 24, 1962, was the Contours' "Do You Love Me." Nationally, it was Bobby "Boris" Pickett's "Monster Mash."

THE NO. 1 HIT ON RADIO MOSCOW

That would be the statement, repeated every half-hour on October 24, that the naval blockade would "unleash nuclear war."

WEDNESDAY MORNING

John F. Kennedy held a meeting with his cabinet at 10 AM Robert McNamara told him that the Navy's procedure upon encountering Russian submarines would be to drop "practice depth charges" to get them to surface. Robert Kennedy wrote, later that day, that his brother's "hand went up to his face & covered his mouth and he closed his fist. His eyes were tense, almost gray."

In a flat in London, Sylvia Plath wrote her poem "Cut," with its images of a thumb wound transformed into a military nightmare: "Out of a gap/A million soldiers run/Redcoats, every one."

At the Apollo, Hal Neely, the coordinator of the Brown recording project and James Brown's longtime business partner, possibly assisted by Tom Nola, set up microphones to tape that day's performances on a big rented AMPEX tape machine.

WEDNESDAY AFTERNOON

October 24, 1962, was U.N. Day, and at 3:00 in the afternoon, as the James Brown revue was already well underway, there was a gala concert in the United Nations General Assembly Hall, about four miles southeast of the Apollo. Yevgeni Mravinsky conducted the Leningrad Philharmonic with violinist David Oistrakh, and a gala reception was held for the musicians afterwards, or at least as gala as possible under the circumstances. Secretary-General U Thant, meanwhile, was desperately trying to convince the American and Soviet governments to cool down their aggression for a few weeks; he made a statement to the Security Council that "the very fate of mankind" was at stake.

The Manchurian Candidate played in theaters for the first time.

The Soviet Union launched Sputnik 22, a space probe intended to fly past Mars. As it was going into Earth orbit, it exploded. American "early warning" radar systems in Alaska detected the debris; for a few minutes, NORAD observers thought it was the start of a nuclear ICBM attack. NORAD's Command Post logs for the day are still classified.

WEDNESDAY EVENING

CBS showed a special at 7:30: *The Other Face of Dixie*, about public-school integration in the South. At the Countee Cullen Library at 138th and Lenox in Manhattan, a documentary on lunchroom sit-in demonstrations was screened at 8:00.

In Cambridge, Massachusetts, Rev. Martin Luther King, Jr., spoke at Harvard Law School's Forum on **"The Future of Integration."** Across the street from him, Todd Gitlin and the Harvard peace group Tocsin organized a rally with Stuart Hughes and Barrington Moore, Jr.; both drew over a thousand spectators. "Until the news was broadcast [on Saturday the 27th] that Khrushchev was backing down," Gitlin wrote in *The Sixties*, "the country lived out the awe and truculence and simmering near-panic always implicit in the thermonuclear age."

AMATEUR NIGHT

The crowds to get into James Brown's show at the Apollo stretched around the block, by all reports. Wednesday nights were, and still generally are, amateur nights at the Apollo; the amateurs were always featured at the beginning of the 11:00 show. You'd rub the stump of the "Tree of Hope," someone would announce what song you'd be performing, and you'd have a cruel and hungry audience waiting for you. If you were less than stellar, it was the hook for you—the comedy "stagehand" Porto Rico would chase you off the stage. If you were Sarah Vaughan or Ruth Brown, winning at amateur night was the first step to stardom. If you weren't, it didn't generally make much of a difference. But the amateur night audiences were screamers—the final show Wednesday would have the most enthusiastic audience response, and the most warmed-up band, of the week.

(There is a long-circulating tale that James Brown competed in amateur night sometime in the '50s, in a shirt and shoes that stage manager Sandman Sims lent him. Brown vehemently denies it in his autobiography, *The Godfather of Soul*, and it does sound like one of those stories that's way too good to be true.)

Immediately before the amateur-night show, at 10:52 PM, President Kennedy's staff read him a cable from Premier Khrushchev, to the effect that the American blockade was "an act of aggression which pushes mankind toward the abyss of a world nuclear-missile war," and that he would not tell Soviet ships to comply with it. Meanwhile, the Strategic Air Command went to DEFCON 2, the highest level of military alert it had ever reached; DEFCON 1 would have been nuclear war.

STAR TIME

Live at the Apollo begins *in medias res*, cutting into the middle of a speech. "So now ladiesangennamen it is *star time* are you ready for STAR *TIME*?" announces Lucas "Fats" Gonder, the James Brown Orchestra's organist and the show's emcee. At this point, the show has already been going on for a good hour or so. "Star time" doesn't mean "seeing James Brown for the first time"—he's already spent quite a bit of time on stage—it means the part of the show where he comes up front and sings.

Here's what probably happened in that night's late show between the amateur-night feature and Star Time (suggested by Alan Leeds' copious notes):

The James Brown Orchestra almost certainly opened the show with a short instrumental set—songs like "Suds" (a composition credited to drummer Nat Kendrick, featuring a ringing guitar hook from Les Buie) and "Night Flying." Sometimes Brown played on the band's instrumental recordings, sometimes he didn't, but they tended to appear on albums with titles like *James Brown Presents His Band and Five Other Great Artists*. The opening set, though, would have been the band playing without Brown, which they still do even now. The band was on a riser at the back of the stage, in two tiers. The front of the riser was decorated with a musical staff, with notes running all the way across it; the horn section (trumpeters Lewis Hamlin, Jr., Roscoe Patrick and Teddy Washington, saxophonists William Burgess, Al "Brisco" Clark, Clifford "Ace King" MacMillan and St. Clair Pinckney, and trombonist Dicky Wells) stood behind waist-high music stands with pictures of saxophones on them. Hamlin, who was celebrating his 32nd birthday that day, was the musical director of the band in those days—the 1990 CD of LATA misspells his name as "Louis Hamblin."

The Orchestra was followed by the Brownies, a dancing chorus who'd joined the revue in September 1961, before which they'd been called the Hortense Allen Dancers. At the time of the Apollo show, they included Helen Riley, Rusty Williams and Pat Perkins, and probably a couple of others; there's a publicity photo of them wearing feathered headdresses, feathered right (but not left) wristbands, feathered bikini bottoms and feathered boots, along with bikini tops that are some kind of advanced (but featherless) sartorial disaster. They're posed in front of a Mondrian-style geometrical backdrop, grinning like they're in on a secret. The picture is captioned in awkward Letraset lettering: "THE BROWN IES DANCING DOLLS FEAT WITH JAMES BROWN SHOW." (The Brownies don't appear to be the same people as the Brownettes, who recorded a JB-produced single a few years later.)

Then James Brown himself came on and sat in for a few instrumentals with the band, first on organ (starting with "Mashed Potatoes U.S.A.," a single that had been released earlier in October), then on drums ("Doin' the Limbo" and "Choo-Choo (Locomotion)"). The Apollo held a dance contest during this segment of the show; there exists a single, blurry photograph of it, with three sharply dressed teenagers doing the mashed potatoes at the front of the stage, while the rhythm section grooves and the horn players look expectantly at Brown, who's sitting at the organ.

Several hundred miles away, President Kennedy called Robert McNamara, who assured him that U.S. armed forces would be ready to invade Cuba in seven days.

THE VALENTINOS

The Valentinos were the new kids on the bill, and probably got to play a three-song set. They were on the front lines of the transition from gospel to R&B that was happening in the late '50s and early '60s. Bobby, Cecil, Curtis, Friendly, Jr. and Harris Womack had first recorded in June 1961—a gospel session under the name the Womack Brothers, with Sam Cooke producing for his label SAR Records. (Cooke had famously made the gospel-to-pop switchover a few years before.) Curtis Womack sang a version of Roscoe Robinson's "Somewhere There's a God," which Cooke promptly rewrote as "Somewhere There's a Girl," and sang with the Womacks backing him up; guitarist Bobby Womack roared the lead part on his own "Couldn't Hear Nobody Pray."

When they came back to record with Cooke again in February 1962, they'd changed their name to the

Valentinos, and they were ready to cut secular material. They remade their own songs—"Somewhere There's a Girl" and a rewritten, sped-up version of "Couldn't Hear Nobody Pray" called "Lookin' For a Love." Released as the Valentinos' first single in July, "Lookin' For a Love" tickled the lower regions of the pop charts, and made No. 8 R&B. (A 1974 re-recording of "Lookin' For a Love" became Bobby Womack's biggest solo hit.)

The Apollo gig was part of the Valentinos' first secular tour; Daniel Wolff's Sam Cooke biography *You Send Me* quotes Curtis remembering "gospel-rockin' the Apollo, using the hang time in the middle of 'Lookin' For a Love' to come forward and get the house." In a November 1975 interview with *Soul and Jazz* magazine, Bobby recalled:

Sam (Cooke) booked us in the Apollo with James Brown, and he sent us $3,000 to buy a car so we could get there ... All the way to New York things kept going wrong, and we had to push the car towards the end, but we got there.

First thing that happened after we checked in at the Cecil Hotel, where all the gospel groups stayed, we ran into this white chick. Now Dad had always warned us about white women, but we were feeling pretty big, being in New York hitting on this white chick. She said she would give us all some action, but it would cost ten dollars. So we took her up to the room, and the next day we all had the clap.

It was a crazy week. We were doing great at the Apollo, but we'd run out of money and didn't know enough to ask for a draw. So we hadn't eaten in three days and were so sick from the clap we could hardly sing. Finally we went to a clinic. Man, we learned a lot that week!

The second time we played the Apollo was with Sam, because he didn't think James Brown had looked after us right.

Sam Cooke played at the Apollo two weeks after the Brown revue; he's rumored to have been in the audience the night LATA was recorded. That's certainly possible, since he was in Europe at the beginning of the week but returned to see the Valentinos' show, according to Wolff. And Cooke would definitely have stuck around to see the headliner: at the beginning of August, he'd produced the Simms Twins' gospel-inflected cover of Brown's 1959 non-hit "Good Good Lovin'."

YVONNE FAIR

Since 1960, there's almost always been a featured female vocalist with the James Brown show; for most of 1962, that singer was Yvonne Fair, a 20-year-old R&B singer from Virginia. The October 20 issue of the *Amsterdam News* ran a publicity photo of her (posed like a Greek statue in a tight dress and spike heels, smiling, one knee lifted a bit, gesturing with her hands as if holding a large trophy); the caption claimed that she was "a native New Yorker and attended Janes Addams Vocational High" (*sic*). James Brown had produced and played on three singles for her that year, notably "I Found You," which he'd remake a few years later as "I Got You (I Feel Good)."

At the time of the Apollo show, Yvonne's latest single was a cover of Gene Allison's 1958 hit "You Can Make It If You Try," reworked with a little sermonette at the beginning. Brown plays the organ on the single, as well as yelling constant encouragement; he might have turned up on stage to play it with her, too. King ran an ad in *Billboard* that month, with a picture of a grinning James Brown in front of a map of the U.S. In banner type, it read "JAMES BROWN and his Famous Flames - AN ALL U.S.A. Hit - King 5672 - MASHED POTATOES U.S.A." Down at the bottom, in much smaller type: "DON'T FORGET - You Can Make It If You Try - It Hurts To Be In Love - Yvonne Fair - King 5687."

What else might she have sung in her three-song spotlight? Maybe "Say So Long," or "If I Knew," from her earlier singles. At least one of her songs, though, was probably a cover of some then-current R&B hit; James Brown has always had an unfortunate habit of making people in his revue with perfectly good repertoires of their own do Motown or Stax karaoke.

Photographer Gordon Anderson made a montage of pictures he took at that week's Apollo shows. Yvonne Fair appears three times in it, including a big cameo-shaped image in its center. She's wearing a blonde wig, for some reason, and a dress with a complicated print. Her makeup makes thick-rimmed almonds of her eyes. In one picture, she's looking up and to one side, her lips pursed, making a little wish. The middle photo is positioned so she looks like she's looking at her other image, smiling professionally but ruefully.

In any case, the night after *Live at the Apollo* was recorded was the last time Yvonne Fair sang on stage to James Brown's audience, because of something she wasn't about to tell them.

FREDDIE KING

1961 had been Texas-born blues guitarist/singer Freddie, or Freddy, King's *annus mirabilis*. He'd placed six songs in the R&B charts (three of them, and one other single, went pop, too)—all released on King Records' subsidiary Federal, maybe so that nobody would think that Syd Nathan's label belonged to a blues guitarist! He never had another hit, but the chitlin circuit took care of its own: once you'd established your name on the network of little venues where black musicians played to mostly black audiences, you could keep playing there forever. That's essentially what King did until his death in 1976—he had, and still has, a cult following among hardcore blues buffs, but is little remembered otherwise.

King's singles usually had a blues vocal on one side and an instrumental on the other—he tried to showcase both sides of his talent whenever possible. The Apollo's ad that week listed his relatively recent single "I'm On My Way To Atlanta" under his name. His three-song set probably included "Hide Away," his long-lived instrumental hit, featuring a bridge that quotes the "Peter Gunn" theme (a riff that the Apollo audience would be hearing a bit later that night, too), and either the instrumental "San-Ho-Zay" or the jaunty blues "I'm Tore Down," which let him both sing and play guitar.

At around the same time that Freddie King was playing "Hide Away," a B-52 bomber took off from Westover Air Force Base in Massachusetts, heading north. The plane had nuclear bombs on board; the understanding was that it was to head over the North Pole and drop them on Russia, unless it got the order to turn back.

SOLOMON BURKE

Solomon Burke's career has matched Brown's for longevity, if not for glory. He'd been appearing at the Apollo Theater in various capacities since the '50s (when

Apollo Records released his first few records, credited to the "Boy Preacher"); he'd had R&B hits with "Just Out of Reach" in 1961 and "Cry To Me" in early 1962, and had spent July touring the South with Brown and his group. "Down in the Valley," its flip side "I'm Hanging Up My Heart For You" and "I Really Don't Want To Know" all hovered around the lower reaches of the pop charts that summer. The ad for the Apollo shows that appeared in the *Amsterdam News* credits him with singing "Tonight My Heart Is Crying," by which it probably means "Cry To Me," rather than the 1957 Shirley Bassey song that Burke never recorded. He most likely sang three songs, too.

PIGMEAT MARKHAM & CO.

Comedian Dewey "Pigmeat" Markham started playing at the Apollo in the '30s and never stopped—he appeared there more than any other act. (A vaudeville performer of the old school, he continued to perform in blackface right up into the '50s.) Curiously, he cut a live album at the Apollo the same week as James Brown. Chess Records recorded Markham's performances on Saturday and Sunday, October 20 and 21, and got six sketches out of it, which ended up being released on his album *The World's Greatest Clown*: "Go Ahead and Sing," "Frisco Kate," "Miss Monzell," "Hello

Bill," "Ritz Service" and "Restaurant Scene." We can assume that those were from six different performances—the *Amsterdam News* plug for the show notes that Markham and crew would present "two comedy sketches, one the very popular 'judge' scene."

That would be the "Here Comes the Judge" routine that was Markham's greatest hit. It first turned up on record in 1961 or so—"The Judge," as it was then called, appeared on his early album *Pigmeat Markham at the Party*. In 1968, Markham broke out to the American mainstream with a series of appearances on the TV comedy show *Laugh-In*, where "Here come the judge!" became a catchphrase. Soul singer Shorty Long adapted "Here Comes the Judge" into a hit funk single that May (No. 4 R&B); Markham, not about to let anyone steal his fire, recorded a danceable "Here Come the Judge" of his own, which followed it up the charts in June (No. 4 R&B, No. 19 pop), as did versions by the Magistrates and the Buena Vistas.

Then: Star Time.

STAR TIME

But back a moment to "Fats" Gonder's introduction, all one-minute-on-the-button of it. It's his star turn before Star Time, and he works it like a carnival barker, throwing in five-dollar turns of phrase but dropping vowels to talk more country. "Thank you, and thank you very kindly. It is indeed a great pleasure to present to you at THIS partic'lar time—national and *inter*national known—as the HHHardest Workin' Man in Show Binness—"

THE HARDEST WORKING MAN IN SHOW BUSINESS

You thought that was just a slogan. *Live at the Apollo* was at least James Brown's *twenty-fourth* show of that week. The Apollo Theater had four or sometimes even five shows a day, starting in the early afternoon, and the revue had been playing there since Friday the 19th. At that point, and through most of the '60s, the James Brown revue was playing around three hundred days a year. (Three hundred days a year. Four or five shows a day.) No venue was too tiny, no drive between gigs that was physically possible to make was too long. This particular leg of their endless tour had started October 9, at the Rainbow Gardens in Denver, Colorado. They worked their way across Texas, then stopped off for a one-off engagement at a gymnasium in Jackson, Mississippi, before the Apollo gigs.

Thursday, October 18, was evidently spent rehearsing in New York. (Trombonist Dicky Wells, a veteran of Count Basie's orchestra, had been brought into the band specifically for the Apollo shows.) Traditionally, the outgoing and incoming shows would have a Thursday-night "wrap party" at the Palm Cafe, a bar and restaurant down the street from the Apollo; between midnight and 3 AM, Major Robinson would broadcast over WWRL from the Palm, although the 18th was his final night there. The show that had just closed at the Apollo had been a gospel revue, featuring the Soul Stirrers (Sam Cooke's former group, who were still among the biggest stars of gospel) and the Swanee Quintet (friends of Brown's from Augusta, Georgia).

After *Live at the Apollo* was recorded, the Brown revue wandered up and down the East Coast, playing armories and arenas, darting west to play at an Odd Fellows Hall in Steubenville, Ohio, on October 30, then spending November in the mid-Atlantic, including ten-day engagements in Baltimore's Royal Theater and Washington, D.C.'s Howard Theater.

By modern standards, James Brown's tour promotions were pretty haphazard. Posters advertising his shows would often say "tickets available in the usual places": record stores, barber shops, drugstores. The Brown organization tended to promote shows themselves, or co-promoted them with local DJs. A smart move: the DJs would get part of the take, so they'd plug the show on the air and play James Brown records whenever they could. This was not really considered an ethical problem in those days. (King Records used to deduct their payola costs as a declared business expense. "Some [DJs] wanted cash only," Syd Nathan said in 1959, "but I told them if they wanted payola they'd have to take a check.")

THE BUS

Never one to pass up free advertising, Brown covered the sides of his revue's 50-passenger tour bus with plugs for every act it carried. His own name appeared biggest of all below the back window, with a little sign below it that read "TRY ME" "BEWILDERED" "YOU'VE GOT THE POWER" "PLEASE, PLEASE, PLEASE." Under the driver's side window was the contact information for his booking agency, Universal Attractions.

On December 7, 1962, the bus was destroyed in an accident in Hagerstown, Maryland—James Brown wasn't on board, but a few members of the band were injured. (Brown generally skipped the bus and drove ahead to wherever the next gig was in his Cadillac, in order to do promotional interviews and plug his records at every radio station within range of the venue.) The accident only knocked out a few dates before their scheduled vacation; everybody got 17 days off before they resumed the endless string of one-nighters with a gig at a high school auditorium in Florence, South Carolina.

THE CATALOGUE OF HITS

Fats Gonder ramps up his delivery from a salesmanlike incantation to rabid enthusiasm. He's got a singer to sell. What's the man he's introducing done with all that hard work? "Man that sang, 'I Go CRAZY'!" The snare smacks as the horn section blares a G chord. It's really "I'll Go Crazy," but Gonder's determined to out-country JB's enunciation. "Try ME!" G-sharp. "YOU've Got the Power!" A. "THINK!" A-sharp. "If You Want Me!" B—except, oh dear, problem in the trumpet section, either Teddy Washington or Mack Johnson hits a bad note. (What was this "If You Want Me"? Not a hit, really—it had been the flip-side of "Bewildered." What was it doing in the list of hits? It sounded good.) "I Don't Mind!" C. "Be-WIL-dered!" C-sharp. (At this point, there's what sounds like the first bit we've lost from the tape—just a tiny dropout, but perhaps there was something edited out there.) "Million-dolla sella 'LOST Someone'!" Not just a million-seller, mind you, but a million-*dollar* seller, at a time when a single usually cost 79 cents. "Lost Someone" had been a No. 2 R&B hit, but given that it only got up to No. 48 on the pop charts, that particular distinction is unlikely. The band hits a D. "The very latest release, 'NIGHT Train'!" Well, no—"Shout and Shimmy" and "Mashed Potatoes U.S.A." had come out since "Night Train"—but it had been his biggest hit that year. D-sharp. "It's everybody 'Shout and SHIMMY'!" We'll be hearing more about that in a minute. E.

GOLD

"Brown has perhaps a dozen 'gold' records to his credit," the little unbylined puff piece in that week's *New York Amsterdam News* announced. That was pushing it—he'd only had 15 chart singles by that point. James Brown didn't have a certified gold single until 1972's "Get On the Good Foot," although King evidently didn't bother with RIAA gold and platinum certification. Still, for an Apollo audience, Gonder had a lot of familiar song titles to mention.

There are an awful lot of citations of chart numbers and dates in this book. Live with them. They are an essential part of James Brown's art. His genius is the genius of rolls of tickets torn off one by one, of money handed over for records, of the *hit*. The great James Brown songs are popular, the popular James Brown songs are great. As George W.S. Trow wrote in another, darker context, "It's a Hit! Love it! It's a Hit. It loves you because you love it because it's a Hit!" "You come to see my show," Brown sang. "That's why James Brown loves you so." "This is a *hit!*," he declared as the tape rolled for "Papa's Got a Brand New Bag"; he cut it out of the released record, but persuaded some of the other artists whose records he produced around that time to yell the same thing, so it might work its magic for them too.

Look at his singles discography, and ignore the instrumentals, the duets, the reissues, the throwaways on King's subsidiary label Bethlehem, the Christmas and novelty records—just concentrate on the songs he threw his weight behind. A pattern emerges, or rather an unbroken block: between "Money Won't Change You" in July 1966 and "Hot (I Need To Be Loved, Loved, Loved, Loved)" nine years later, James Brown had over *sixty consecutive* chart hits. On his own terms, he was an unstoppable champion, and those terms were people paying to hear him sing, and being reassured that what they were paying for was *popular*.

That's why he wanted to make *Live at the Apollo* so badly: he could demonstrate that being James Brown was *itself* a hit. All he had to do was get it on tape.

THE CATALOGUE OF HITS

Back at the Apollo, Gonder's speech has been setting up a couple of subliminal effects. Starting with "You've

Got the Power," and running through "Bewildered," there's a steady 6/8 rhythm to the words he accents and the band's stabs—a tick-tock swing that's at pretty much the same tempo as Brown's ballads. There's also a hidden message in those emphases—Crazy-Me-You-Think-Want-Mind-Be-WILL-Lost-Night-Shimmy! This is a night for total abandon, the suggestion goes; for thoughts to become desires and then to simply be, through sheer will; a night to be lost to shimmying.

(A young man named Danny Ray was waiting in the wings. He'd just been hired, that week, as James Brown's valet; a few years later, he'd take over the emcee job, which he still holds today, and his introductions to the James Brown show have been patterned on Gonder's ever since.)

Gonder's still going. "Mr. Dynamite"—*Mr. Dynamite* had been the title of two movies, one from 1935, adapted from Dashiell Hammett's story "On the Make," and the other from 1941, starring Lloyd Nolan as Tommy N. Thornton (nice initials)—"the amazing Mr. Please, Please himself, the star of the show"—as if there could be any doubt, as Gonder is almost erupting with conviction—"JAMES BROWN AND the FAMOUS FLAMES!"

THE SCRATCH

The horns buck—one, two, three, four, five, all on a G chord that's climbed up an octave since Gonder started his litany. It's the beginning of a fanfare to announce the Hardest Working Man In Show Business's arrival: three choruses of a perky little blues riff. Brown glides onto stage during the third, and probably does some high-powered footwork, judging by the screams. Twenty-nine years old and as flexible as a piece of yarn, he can dance faster and harder than anyone, rippling his body, floating over a wooden floor as if it's water-slicked ice.

The perky little blues riff has a name, although it was never credited on any edition of *Live at the Apollo* until 2004: it's "The Scratch." Brown and his band (including Les Buie on guitar and Hubert Perry on bass, still with the band at the Apollo) had recorded it as an instrumental on October 4, 1960. ("The Scratch" is also a close cousin of Henry Mancini's "Peter Gunn" theme, which had been a hit for Ray Anthony in 1959; Duane Eddy's version charted for the first time on October 10, 1960.) Brown's version appeared as the B-side of "Hold It" in January 1961, and the band played it as his entrance music at least through mid-1963.

As the band bats down the last note again and again, you can almost see James Brown's feet slide frictionlessly into position behind the microphone.

I'LL GO CRAZY

James Brown steps up to the front of the Apollo stage, gazes out over 1500 thoroughly warmed-up faces, and assesses matters with a huge holler. He feels all right, and he wants to make sure everybody knows it. The third time he announces it, he gives the "all" an enormous melismatic rush, swooping around at least twelve notes just to prove he can; then, as he takes a breath, guitarist Les Buie whacks sharply at his strings, and we're into "I'll Go Crazy."

THE MISSING SONG

Except we're not: there's almost certainly at least one song missing from the set on *Live at the Apollo*. In those days, JB usually opened his shows with his latest hit. In October 1962, that was "Shout and Shimmy," which had made No. 16 on the R&B chart (No. 61 pop) back in August. Recorded February 9, 1961 (the same day as "Lost Someone" and "Night Train"), it starts with the I-feel-all-right routine, and then proceeds to a truly shameless ripoff of the Isley Brothers' 1959 hit "Shout."

(Really, truly shameless. The "I feel all right" business is derived from the beginning of the second half of the Isleys' record, and the rest of the record is basically the fast parts of "Shout," with the gospel inflections removed and the word "shimmy" added. It wasn't the last time JB would appropriate the Isleys' work as his own, either: "It's My Thing," his protégée Marva Whitney's 1969 single, credited to J. Brown/M. Whitney, could be charitably described as an answer song to the Isleys' "It's Your Thing." It could be less charitably described as a cover that changes the pronouns.)

Those who wonder what "Shout and Shimmy" might have sounded like here are directed to the chaotic live follow-up album *Pure Dynamite!* (recorded, for the most part, at the Royal Theatre in Philadelphia in 1963 and released in 1964; it'll be discussed more later on). It mostly covers the part of Brown's concert repertoire that hadn't ended up on *Live at the Apollo*; "Shout and Shimmy" opens the show with a minute and a half of thunderous frenzy, followed by a strange little sing-speech on which Brown declares "I'm tired but I'm clean" and goofs around with a comedian.

Why was "Shout and Shimmy" omitted from *Live at the Apollo*? Alan Leeds suggests that it might have been excised at the request of King Records president Syd Nathan, who was uneasy enough about the live album as it was, and might not have wanted it to compete with the song's studio incarnation. It might also be that the performance didn't seem quite appropriate for the beginning of an album—the *Pure Dynamite* version sure doesn't.

There might be more missing from the *Apollo* performance, in fact. "This album is the actual recording of the midnight show and includes the actual 40 minutes of James Brown on stage," Hal Neely wrote in his liner notes to the original album. But *Live at the Apollo* is under 32 minutes long—a little bit skimpy for Star Time. Maybe Gonder was mentioning "If You Want Me" because JB intended to sing it (although it's one of his vaguest, most unconvincing ballads). Maybe Brown also sang "I've Got Money," a wild rocker that he'd recorded back in May, although the single wouldn't see release for a few weeks yet. Or maybe "Please, Please, Please" was abridged, for reasons that will be explained later.

This is all guesswork. As far as Leeds and Polygram Records' Harry Weinger know, none of the outtake material still exists. In 1971, James Brown moved from King Records to the much bigger label, Polydor, and took his back catalogue's master tapes with him; King subsequently sold its archive to Gusto Records in Nashville. There are rumors that a box or two accidentally ended up in Gusto's vault in 1971, but that's not likely, and Gusto's not talking. The 2000 fire that destroyed the offices of James Brown Enterprises in Augusta, Georgia, was sometimes reported to have burned the master tapes of an Apollo concert, but almost certainly not this one. And the outtakes, if they existed, were probably not stored by Brown: "During the time I worked for Brown in Cincinnati (1969–1971) and Augusta (1971–1973), I never saw or heard any evidence that suggested he had any substantial collection of tape in his homes or businesses," Leeds writes.

In any case, it's a smart edit. The introduction to "Shout and Shimmy" dovetails neatly with "I'll Go Crazy"; the flow of the show might have been imperfect in real life, but you'd never guess it from the way the album fits together. *Live at the Apollo* was edited by Gene Redd, a big-band trumpeter who'd gone on to be a staff producer at King Records—he'd played on a couple of Freddie King's sessions, in fact. Redd later edited a few more James Brown live albums: *Live at the Garden* (1967) and *Live at the Apollo, Vol. II* (1968).

I'LL GO CRAZY

James hasn't even started singing yet, and the crowd is already shrieking—maybe he's executing one of his improbable dance moves. The rhythm section is swinging into something like the 6/8-time ballads that were Brown's bread and butter through the late '50s, except they're playing this one fairly fast and very hard, with Clayton Fillyau bashing at the cymbal on every single beat. The trumpet blasts at the end of the intro are more enthusiastic than accurate, as JB reaches for the microphone. (He'd never just stand in front of the mic—he always has one hand on it, as a sign of intimacy.) The snare and cymbal detonate six times, rushing the beat just enough to suggest that something too exciting to wait for is about to happen.

(Incidentally, there's a longstanding debate over whether or not Clayton Fillyau was the only drummer at the Apollo shows: Brown often toured with two drummers, although his old standby Nat Kendrick didn't rejoin the group until mid-November. The CD edition of LATA lists Sam Latham as an additional drummer, but it turns out he didn't join the band until 1963. The one extant photo of the full band at the Apollo engagement—that blurry dance-contest shot—has two drum kits in it, one on a riser behind the other. Fillyau's playing the front kit, and the back kit is empty. George Sims, from Greensboro, North Carolina, may have been the second drummer.)

The band cuts out for a second, and Brown's voice erupts. "If you leave me," he sings, accusatorily, and the well-dressed men behind him on the stage echo him: "leave meeee!"

FLAMES

This is the first we've heard from the Famous Flames. Contrary to popular belief, the Flames weren't JB's backup band—they were his backup singers. The lineup of Famous Flames varied over the years, although they almost always included Bobby Byrd. The others present for the Apollo gig were Eugene "Baby Lloyd" Stallworth and Bobby Bennett. Both had originally joined the group in 1959, having initially been hired as valets for Brown and for his then-bandleader J.C. Davis, respectively. Stallworth was replaced by first-generation Flame Johnny Terry (who'd served time and sung with James Brown in Georgia Juvenile Training Institute, and was credited with co-writing "Please, Please, Please") in early 1962, and replaced him in turn a few weeks before the Apollo shows. The group, in one form or another, continued to appear on stage with Brown through the '60s, but "Maybe the Last Time," released less than two years after LATA was recorded, was the last James Brown studio recording that featured them.

Stallworth made occasional half-hearted attempts at a solo career, though always as a Brown hanger-on. "Baby Lloyd" was one of the featured performers on the revue's July 1962 tour of the South, before he rejoined the Famous Flames proper; *The James Brown*

Show, a 1966 recording of Brown's entourage, features Stallworth's nondescript performances of "(I Can't Get No) Satisfaction" and Rufus Thomas's "The Dog," spruced up by the high-powered band. He even got two singles of his own: "I Need Love (I've Got Money)" in 1960 (Brown would do much better by it two years later), and a verbatim imitation of Bobby Marchan's hit variation on Big Jay McNeely's "There Is Something On Your Mind."

A record credited solely to the Famous Flames didn't appear until the end of 1970—a pretty good one-off deep-soul single, "Who Am I," written and primarily sung by Johnny Terry, who was basically never heard from again. Bobby Byrd, though, was the Flame who got to emerge, at least partly, from James Brown's shadow. More on him later.

I'LL GO CRAZY

"I'll Go Crazy," recorded November 11, 1959, at the same session as the minor hit "This Old Heart," had originally been Brown's first single of 1960 (it made No. 15 on the R&B chart). It's a little sleepy in its studio incarnation. You can't say that about the live version, which revs the tempo up considerably—Les Buie detonates every note of his lead guitar part, and James Brown is springing off the faithful Flames like a diving board. They've had to attenuate what they're singing to keep up, too—the "oh yeah"s on the original recording become a crisp little "oyp!" here.

The other big difference, though, is that on the studio recording, JB is decidedly singing a lyric—a very simple lyric, but still a piece of text with a meaning. Here, he's often just showing off what his voice can do: alternating between an R&B shout and a rough croon (isolate every time he sings "I'll go crazy" in your head, and it sounds like he's singing the emphatic parts of a slow, quiet song rather than swinging and belting), leaping up to yelp, getting so caught up in the performance that he strays from the microphone on the second bridge: "You gotta live for yourself . . . yeah? AAAA! . . . eeee, I'll go crazy . . . " The madness is starting to come over him.

MADNESS

James Brown screams and sweats and implores. His path is a jagged slash. He flies off the text of the song, flits from one song to another, begins and ends when he pleases. As long as he works hard and can be seen working hard, he is almost unbounded by the responsibility of sticking to the program. Nobody else in his band can even break a sweat: they are required to work impossibly hard, too, but they are not to be seen with a hair out of place. James Brown is a vector of chaos, and chaos only means something by comparison with order. So the rest of his band is architecturally orderly, shoes shined and suits crisp, holding steady while he plays with phrasing, beats, song structure. They're at his mercy.

The Famous Flames become the voices in the head of a madman. He argues with them, or lets them complete his thoughts. "I'll Go Crazy" is the first statement here of his great theme: *you must not leave him*. If he stops commanding your attention, the craziness that makes him yowl and moan will consume everything. But, of course, the bridge of the song (where the Flames do more singing than he does) slyly adds, do what you like, you can't live for him.

It would be possible to sing "I'll Go Crazy" in a genuinely abject, desperate way—and we'll hear plenty of that kind of singing later—but that's not how Brown sings it. His singing here is flashy, even cocky, as if he's toying with the object of the song, daring her to leave him so he can demonstrate just how crazy he can be. There's a cruel, devouring side to both his madness and his need.

As James Brown swings the microphone back toward himself, a bulky, shadowy figure climbs the security fence at an Air Force base in Duluth, Minnesota. A guard shoots at it; thinking that it might be a saboteur, he sets off an alarm.

I'LL GO CRAZY

The Apollo version of "I'll Go Crazy," with a verse and "you gotta live" bridge repeated to pad it out to a more single-like two minutes and ten seconds, was released as the B-side of "Lost Someone" (edited down from the LATA recording) in early 1966. The live "Lost Someone" went to No. 94 on the pop chart; "I'll Go Crazy" was No. 38 R&B and No. 73 pop. They may have ridden the coattails of Brown's previous single, the massive smash "I Got You (I Feel Good)," but it's still not a bad performance for two chopped-up live tracks in a style he'd almost abandoned by that point.

ABANDONING STYLES

"The King of the One-Nighters" was one of his nicknames, and the Apollo was as good as the chitlin circuit got, but James Brown was already aspiring to move beyond it. LATA was, arguably, meant as Brown's farewell to the raw R&B phase of his career; less than two months later, he was recording "Prisoner of Love" with an orchestra and chorus. Ray Charles had started a long series of string-sweetened country crossover hits in May 1962, driven by songs from his smash album *Modern Sounds in Country & Western Music*. JB had followed the example of Charles's live album *In Person*; now he wanted credit in the pop world as a balladeer. The

Prisoner of Love album included versions of "Try Me" and "Lost Someone," with strings added for the easy-listening audience.

It didn't quite work: he couldn't entirely pull off the lounge act, and the "new direction" of his career got derailed by a record-company mess that took up most of the next few years. By the time he got back into the swing of things, it was 1965, and his breakthrough record was the distinctly un-smooth "Papa's Got a Brand New Bag." But it took him a long time to give up on the crossover dream: in 1968 and 1969, he recorded albums with a cocktail jazz trio and the Louie Bellson Orchestra, and played the International Hotel in Las Vegas, singing "If I Ruled the World" and "September Song." Again, it failed to catch on. His subsequent foray into acid-rock was even shorter: a pretty good single (the original version of "Talkin' Loud and Sayin' Nothing"), which was withdrawn almost immediately, and an awful instrumental album, *Sho Is Funky Down Here*.

TRY ME

Back at the Apollo, the horn riff at the end of "I'll Go Crazy" slows down and slides perfectly into the first word of "Try Me"—a flawless key change with no audible cue, the kind of trick JB will be pulling off throughout the show. That word, "try," is all the girls up front need to start screaming like a descending horde of locusts.

That instant recognition has to have been a relief for James Brown. "Please, Please, Please" had been a hit, but its follow-up singles weren't. Nine flops in a row came out in 1956, 1957 and 1958; Brown lost his original band and his original Flames as his name failed to appear on chart after chart. After an October 1957 session, King Records pretty much gave up recording him.

(Consider for a moment what might have happened if James Brown had left the music business at the end of his 2 1/2-year losing streak. Somebody might have put out a retrospective CD in the '90s, when all sorts of R&B obscurities were getting reissued; "Just Won't Do Right" and the B-side "Messing With the Blues" might even have been played a few times on specialty radio shows.)

"Try Me" probably saved his career. Released in October 1958, after radio play for Brown's own demo convinced King's Syd Nathan to record it for real, it was his first No. 1 R&B hit, and stayed on the Top 100 for 22 weeks (longer than any other Brown single *ever* has), even making it to No. 14 on the pop chart. "I had heard 'Raindrops' by Dee Clark and 'For Your Precious

Love' by Jerry Butler and the Impressions," he notes in his autobiography, "so I wrote my song to fit between them."

Well, that's one possible story of where "Try Me" comes from, but it's not exactly in Brown's songwriting style. "James found the song down in Florida while he was working The Palms in Hallandale," Bobby Byrd told interviewer Cliff White. "I'm pretty sure it was really written by some other guy who just gave it away to James to record; either that or James developed it out of something he heard down there."

A January 1961 article in *Sepia* magazine by Stella Comeaux, most of which appears to be totally fictional, suggests a third origin for "Try Me":

> "A scout for the Chicago White Sox once tried to sign me up for their farm team," James explained. "But about this time I met a man named Andy Gibson—now my repertoire man. He tried me out with the song 'Try Me' and that was it. Andy told me I had what it took to become a top singer. That was good enough for me. He has been handling my music and arranging ever since."

Andy Gibson was a songwriter, arranger and producer at King Records; he'd co-written the much-covered Paul Williams hit "The Hucklebuck," produced the "Try Me" session, and co-wrote a couple of songs with Brown under his pseudonym Albert Shubert.

Here's Brown on Gibson's role in the making of "Try Me," in *The Godfather of Soul*: "Andy stayed out of my way, and that's what I wanted."

Wherever the song came from, it worked. "Try Me" was a minor hit for Brown again in 1965, this time as an organ-led instrumental (No. 34 R&B, No. 63 pop). He was apparently convinced for a while that it could work for anyone in his circle, too. The short-lived 1963 record label that released various JB productions was Try Me Records. In 1966, producing his old friends the Swanee Quintet, he gave them the barely altered "Try Me, Father" (as well as "That's the Spirit," a re-write of his recent hit "Ain't That a Groove"). Gospel singer Kay Robinson got "Try Me, Father" in 1968, too. Wendy Lynn had a one-off single with "Try Me" in 1970. Martha High, who sang with Brown for 27 years, only got one single of her own for the first seven of those years—"Try Me," in 1973. None of them charted.

The LATA version is closer to its studio incarnation than any other song in the show, down to the nearly identical instrumental break (with what sounds like both drummers playing at once). It's a little faster, definitely, but that does good things for the song. After the beginning, the screams largely subside, with intermittent outbreaks. The mix of the band is so precise you can hear the Flames' unison clap on every sixteenth beat, although James's microphone is acting up—it cuts out a couple of times. You can't blame it: he's almost sleepwalking through the performance, at least by his standards, and the band speeds up bit by bit, as if they just want to get to the other end of the hit they always have to play. Even so, "Try Me" is valuable in the context of LATA, because it acts in the service of the album's pace: if "I'll Go Crazy" were followed directly by "Think," it would be practically numbing.

The sabotage alarm in Duluth sets off other alarms at other military locations nearby. At Volk Field in Wisconsin, the alarm that goes off is the wrong one—it's the signal for F-106s, with Falcon air-to-air nuclear missiles, to scramble. At DEFCON 3 or higher, there are no practice alert drills, and the Strategic Air Command had switched to DEFCON 2 that day. As far as the pilots in Wisconsin know, the war has just started.

HOLD IT

Before anybody can breathe, before the applause starts to crest, Les Buie sprays out a little guitar figure, and the band pounces into position: one chorus of a twelve-bar blues riff. This one has a name, too. It's "Hold It," which had been an instrumental hit for Bill Doggett in 1958 (No. 3 R&B, No. 92 pop), written by his guitarist Billy Butler and tenor saxophonist Clifford Scott. Doggett had played with the Ink Spots, Wynonie Harris and Louis Jordan, before becoming a successful band-leader in the early '50s with a series of singles on King Records.

The biggest Doggett hit of all was 1956's "Honky Tonk," another favorite of Brown's. James and the Flames recorded a vocal version of "Honky Tonk" called "Let's Make It"—with writing credit for Brown alone, naturally—in July of that year, before it had become a hit. In 1972, the James Brown Soul Train (basically the entire revue, chanting the title over and over) released a two-part version of "Honky Tonk" that went to No. 7 on the R&B charts. It's also not hard to detect some "Honky Tonk" DNA in Brown's enormous 1973 hit "Doin' It To Death," released under the name Fred Wesley & the J.B.'s. As with so many of Brown's early influences (and King Records acts with ailing careers), Doggett eventually ended up under his disciple's wing: JB produced a smashing 1969 remake of "Honky Tonk" for him, backed with the inevitable "Honky Tonk Popcorn."

A FLASHBACK TO 1959

James Brown was getting his first real taste of stardom after "Try Me," and was already starting to think big. Almost alone among the major R&B singers of the day, he had a high-caliber band that toured with him; earlier that year, leader James Davis had put out a single, "Doo-dle Bug," featuring the group. It had stiffed, but it gave Brown an idea—the James Brown Orchestra was open-ing his shows with instrumental sets, he'd already had three legitimate hits under his own name, so why not use the name and the band to promote each other with some instrumental records?

But King Records' Syd Nathan wasn't having it—he had no interest in throwing good money after bad. So Brown went down to Florida to visit record producer and distributor Henry Stone, who recorded the band lurching through a rudimentary riff. The result was "(Do The) Mashed Potatoes," a No. 8 R&B hit released on Stone's label Dade Records in early 1960 and cred-ited to Nat Kendrick and the Swans (Kendrick was the group's drummer). They followed up with "Dish Rag," "Slow Down" and "Wobble Wobble," none of which was particularly successful. Still, Brown and the crew toured the South as the instrumental-plus-hollering band Nat Kendrick and the Swans, doing the mashed potatoes in roadhouses night after night, building a second career for themselves.

Eventually, Nathan caught on that he had two star acts in one. By October 1960, he'd agreed to let the band cut another instrumental single, "Hold It"/"The

Scratch"; making the A-side a cover of a Doggett tune that had appeared on King a couple of years before might well have been a thank-you to Nathan. This time, it was credited as "James Brown Presents His BAND." So much for the Swans, and so much for Kendrick's star turn. (The drummer on the single version of "Hold It," in fact, is Brown himself—hollering, as usual, from what sounds like a fair distance from the nearest microphone.)

Brown's version tweaks Doggett's a little, though. Where Billy Butler starts the song with a bouncy major-key guitar figure before he hits the seventh chord that underpins most of its riff, guitarist Les Buie changes the opening melody to anticipate the seventh, giving it a sneakier, bluesier feel, both on Brown's studio recording and LATA.

MASHED POTATOES ONE MORE TIME

Twenty years after Syd Nathan brought "Nat Kendrick and the Swans" back from Henry Stone's Dade Records, Brown found himself working with Stone again. He made a 1980 album, *Soul Syndrome*, for Stone's label TK Records, which includes solid, somewhat discofied versions of both "Honky Tonk" and "Mashed Potatoes."

THINK

The first appearance on *Live at the Apollo* of the "Hold It" link is also a pacesetter for the rocketing version of "Think" that follows it—a performance so fast that it can only be meant as a reminder of how fast James Brown's first recording of it seemed.

The "5" Royales, who sang the original version of "Think," were among the great also-rans of R&B history, far more fondly remembered than their limited chart presence would suggest. Led by songwriter/guitarist Lowman Pauling, they started out as a gospel group, the Royal Suns, in 1942, and changed their name to its familiar version when they went secular in 1952. Their harmonies and arrangements continued to be more gospel than doo-wop, and their rhythm section had a snarling R&B edge—James Brown picked up a thing or two from early hits like "Baby Don't Do It."

In 1956, riding the success of "Please, Please, Please," James Brown and the Famous Flames played on a bill with the "5" Royales (as well as B.B. King and Ray Charles) at the Palms of Hallandale, down in Florida. Within a year, the Royales were recording for King, too. (By that time, the quotes around the 5 were justified, since there were now six of them.) The "5" Royales' "Think" hit the charts on August 5, 1957, and eventually reached No. 9 R&B and No. 57 pop. They would have only one more minor hit, in 1961: the much-covered "Dedicated to the One I Love," in a 1957 recording with sweet backup vocals added to capitalize on the success of the Shirelles' version.

Their original "Think" is a magnificent record in a disappearing idiom, exactly the kind of recording Brown would have made in 1957, if he could, while he was struggling with the likes of the novelty song "That Dood It." Pauling's guitar hovers and stabs; the arrangement suspends the diction of its key lines across moments that are abruptly bare except for handclaps and spidery twangs, the sort of trick Brown would pull off dozens of times over the next few decades.

"King Records wanted me to cut ['Think'] in 1960 at the same session I did 'You've Got the Power,'" James Brown claims in his autobiography, "but I didn't want to. I knew that if I did, it would hurt the Five Royales . . . I held off until they cut 'Please, Please, Please,' then I decided it would be all right to cut 'Think.'" That's a nice story, but it doesn't jibe with the facts. James Brown did indeed record his own version of "Think" in February 1960, at the same session as "You've Got the Power." A single with both songs charted May 30, and "Think" got to No. 7 on the R&B chart and No. 33 on the pop chart. The "5" Royales left King Records that year (they have little good to say about Syd Nathan), and found a new home on the tiny Memphis label Home of the Blues; their version of "Please, Please, Please" didn't appear until October.

It's occasionally been reported that the Royales had some sort of legal tussle over Brown's recording of "Think" that led to the schism with King. John Tanner was the "5" Royales' lead tenor in those days, and he says that nothing of the kind happened—they never had any problem with the Brown version. (Pauling, who died in 1974, isn't likely to have objected to the songwriting royalties from a hit cover, either.) As for their recording of "Please, Please, Please," Tanner says, the answer is simple: "He did 'Think,' so we did 'Please'!"

The Royales' version is stately, half-sanctified, swinging; Brown's studio version smacks off all of the original's smooth edges with a spiked club, cranking up the speed, pushing Nat Kendrick's drumming way up to the top of the mix and interpolating a bristling, sore solo by saxophonist J.C. Davis. And Brown's singing is wild-eyed and suspicious—he elongates every key syllable, lagging behind the beat so he can leap out front again, worrying notes until they threaten to wreck the microphone. He called his version "a combination of gospel and jazz"; whatever it was (and it sure didn't sound much like the kind of gospel or jazz that made it onto records), it was his first great dance record, and the singing pointed toward the kind of soul he'd perfect over the next couple of years.

As Brown had expected, the success of his radical update of the Royales' 2 1/2-year-old hit made it clear that his was the new way and theirs was the old. If there was any bad blood between the "5" Royales and Brown, though, it didn't last long. Brown produced Vicki Anderson singing Pauling's "The Feeling Is Real" and "Tears of Joy" in 1967, and Lyn Collins's fabulous funk version of "Baby, Don't Do It" in 1975. A revamped lineup of the Royales even came under the Brown aegis briefly in late 1964—they toured with the revue for almost six months, and two more singles appeared under the simplified name the Five Royals. One had a pair of remakes of their old songs, the other had two new songs credited to "L. Pauling – T. Wright" (Ted Wright was Brown's songwriting alias), and published by Try Me Music. Very much a throwback to their '50s style, the new singles went nowhere, and that was the end of the group; Pauling subsequently became a session guitarist.

In any case, it's inarguable that James Brown loved "Think." He re-recorded it as a duet with Vicki Anderson, featuring a souped-up arrangement in early 1967, and it poked into the pop chart at No. 100 for a week. A similar "Think," this time a duet with Marva Whitney, opened the *Live at the Apollo, Vol. II* album the next year. In May 1973, he had a hit (No. 15 R&B, No. 77 pop) with a slick, discofied version of "Think," sung over a pre-recorded backing track arranged by Dave Matthews (no relation to the later jam-band leader). His next chart appearance (No. 37 R&B, No. 80 pop), two months later, was "Think"—*again*—sung over the same backing track, but namedropping "Soul Train" this time.

"Think"'s for-God's-sake-don't-leave-me lyric is maybe the smartest articulation of his favorite theme that Brown has ever sung. Interestingly, though, there's one verse he has always changed. "How much of all your happiness have I really claimed?" Lowman Pauling's original lyric goes. "How many tears have you cried for which I was to blame?/Darlin', I can't remember which was my fault/I tried so hard to please you—at least that's what I thought."

On LATA, Brown sings it as "How much of your happiness can I really claim?/How many tears have you shed for which you was to blame, now?/Darlin', I don't remember just what is wrong/I tried so hard to please you—at least that's what I thought." Every version he's released is similar. The alterations seem small, but they change the whole meaning of the song. He's not wondering how much of her happiness he *has* claimed—that is, if he's taken the best years of her life—but how much he's entitled to; he's asking how much of her crying is her own damn problem, not how much is his responsibility; and he's not looking for his role in the source of the problem, he's forgetting what the problem itself is. After all, he's done his part.

SWEAT

James Brown is already covered with sweat as he dances across the Apollo's stage to the instrumental break of "Think." His face looks like it's wearing a mask, a huge lattice of tiny diamonds, rolling down his face or just falling off and crashing to the floor. His hair, painstakingly styled before each show by Frank McRae from Philadelphia into a gleaming, processed pompadour, is becoming disheveled; little soaking-wet strands of it fall across his face, tufts are sticking up from the slick black mass. He is wincing as he sings and smiling when he doesn't.

JAMES BROWN ON THE TOPIC OF HAIR AND TEETH, IN HIS AUTOBIOGRAPHY

"Hair is the first thing. And teeth are second. Hair and teeth. A man got those two things he's got it all."

THINK

Standing behind him, James Brown's band are playing their arrangement of "Think" as fast as they're capable of getting through it without collapsing (it almost falls apart during the solo). Through most of the song, JB is skimming across the lyrics like a seabird, touching down on them only now and then. He holds off on the first "Think" as long as it's feasible, and then some—almost all the way through the next phrase of the song. Then he jumps free of the rhythm for a moment: " . . . about the baaaaad things"—and garbles a few vowels for a moment before he sings something a little bit like the first verse. This song cannot possibly make sense to anyone who hasn't already heard it. He's doing to his own record what the record did to the "5" Royales. That? That was two *years* ago. Catch *up*.

(Later in his life, speeding up songs to make them more exciting will become a toxin afflicting James Brown's live shows. "I Got You" and "Papa's Got a Brand New Bag" will turn into thirty-second throwaways; slow, hard funk grooves will be accelerated until they lose their bite. But this one works.)

The Famous Flames just move and clap. They can't possibly keep up with the background vocals, except for the odd snap of "think!" in the chorus. The two drummers are playing so fast their beat almost keeps up with the speed of the organ's oscillations. When the song ends with two bold blue horn clusters, you can imagine the entire band quietly panting. Except for Les Buie, who barely has time to wipe his hands off before he has to start the link.

HOLD IT

Another twelve seconds of "Hold It," another twelve seconds of dancing in radiantly shiny black shoes. (Brown, as he never tires of telling people, was a shoe-shine boy as a child, and has kept the impulse ever since: he'd fine his bandmembers if their shoes were scuffed.) The rest of what James Brown was wearing? It's hard to say: he traveled with around 70 tailored suits, which he called his "uniforms." A February 1962 *Sepia* magazine article featured him showing off his "$50,000 wardrobe" and mentioning that when he did a weeklong engagement in a theater, he'd wear 35 different outfits—a different one for each show.

The band is perfectly groomed, suited-up, in place, hitting cues with near-military precision. If somebody missed a note or played an extra beat, Brown would dance over to them and flash his hand at them—once for five dollars, twice for ten—and dock their pay for that night.

I DON'T MIND

Brown was a disciplinarian, though, not a perfectionist: he had no objection to letting great records go out with bad notes on them. (Check out the guitar solo in the middle of 1971's "Get Up, Get Into It and Get Involved." It's *terrible*, but that was the take with the feeling, so it stayed in.) When he recorded "I Don't Mind" on September 27, 1960, guitarist Les Buie screwed up, coming in slightly too early for his solo; Brown liked the mistake so much he insisted on keeping it. Actually, the entire song has a slight air of off-ness to it. The bunched-up triplet rhythm that leads into every verse tends to speed up, the chord sequence is bizarre, and the Famous Flames are having a rough time trying to keep their place—you can hear them adjusting their notes, moment by moment. (It can't help that they start singing an "oh-oh-oh" for a few bars before the lead singer deigns to join them.) "I don't *mind*," Brown insists; "Idamind!" his Flames chirp back, mockingly. And the "you gonna miss me" that ends every verse is followed by a pregnant gap where the next downbeat is supposed to be. It was appealingly weird enough that it became a hit (No. 4 R&B, No. 47 pop).

The LATA version follows the general blueprint of the studio recording, but accentuates its weirdness. Fats Gonder plays organ rather than piano, which plays up the chords' awkward swerve through sevenths and thir-teenths, the kind of intervals that would form the back-bone of Brown's funk period, starting a few years later. The Flames are a bit more locked into their peculiar backup moans, and switch between wordless vowels ("ohhh," "üüüüü," "eeee") and the response to Brown's "I don't mind" is compressed into something so brief it sounds like an "aua"; Buie reprises his guitar mistake in a studied way. As soon as Brown comes in, there's an all-but-inaudible dispute in the audience—a woman yelps something, a man answers her crossly. The guitar break's sole lyric (an antecedent-less "somewhere down the line") has its mystery deepened by a vocal-mic drop-out that would be unacceptable on a studio recording and appears to turn it into "somewhere I'm down tonight."

The last "you gonna miss me" is answered by a woman in the crowd, yelling encouragement: "I sure do, baby!" This isn't the last time we'll hear her voice on the record. In *The Godfather of Soul*, Brown spins a story about how, when they were test-recording the earliest shows that day, "a little old lady down front kept yelling, 'Sing it motherf_____r, sing it!'" (*sic*), and how the LATA project's coordinator Hal Neely bribed her to stay for the day's remaining shows, but moved the microphone so it couldn't pick her up quite so well. It's a good story, anyway, and Neely tells the same yarn.

But maybe Brown is trying to drown her out, or getting frustrated at how someone might be ruining his expensive live recording: for the "goodbye, so long" right after that, he's almost shrieking. He brings his voice back down quickly—"no no no no"—then swerves away from the mic to sing a last few words and cue the band to end the song.

"I Don't Mind," incidentally, was a particular favorite of the Who in their early days—Roger Daltrey was reportedly a tremendous James Brown fan—and on April 12, 1965, they recorded a faithful if more ornately arranged version of it for their first album, *My Generation* (along with "Please, Please, Please," which made the album too, and "Shout and Shimmy," which ended up as the B-side of the British "My Generation" single).

Out at Volk Field in Wisconsin, somebody in the command post is smart enough to check in with Duluth and find out what had happened. He drives out to the tarmac and gets the nuclear-armed jets to stop before they take off. The "saboteur" on the security fence in Duluth had been a bear.

HOLD IT

Same link, third time—none of them are labeled as "Hold It" on any edition of LATA. On the 1990 CD it's just called "Instrumental Bridge"; on the 2004 reissue it doesn't even get its own track number. Every time the band plays "Hold It" in the Apollo set, it's a tiny bit faster. Those tiny bits added up, it appears. On *Pure Dynamite!*, recorded live less than a year later, "Hold It" shows up again as a blurringly fast link between "These Foolish Things" and "Signed, Sealed and Delivered," obscured by applause but still discernible; the band blazes through the whole theme in eight seconds.

And, as the song speeds up and Les Buie's attack on that pungent seventh chord turns to a light-fingered skitter, it starts to sound like funk—specifically, like the kind of funk James Brown would invent a few years later and perfect in the early '70s, of which that kind of guitar playing is a pillar. It's not there yet, but there's an ancestral resemblance.

The third and last "Hold It" is also the bridge from a good live album to a great performance. Up until this point, *Live at the Apollo* has been a juiced-up run-through of two-minute hit R&B singles. But that was a tour of a showman's catalogue—Fats Gonder's introduction presented the first part of Star Time as the work of a consistent hitmaker. Now we're about to get something very different.

LOST SOMEONE

The introduction to "Lost Someone" is a remarkable bit of rhetoric. JB starts by echoing Fats Gonder's catalogue of his hits, running off the titles of seven songs in a row. This time, though, it's transformed from a list to a narrative—a speech in his chief mode of argument, the don't-leave-me line he's been working since "Please, Please, Please." Gonder got rising blasts of excitement with each new title he announced: for James Brown himself, the horns don't climb. They stay in the same place, and slap him down, bam bam!, every time he cries out. He is wounded but impossible to stop. His songs are the articulation of his need, the elaboration of his great theme, the definition of a man on the verge of abandonment. His declaration of abjection will not be denied. He is bewildered, crushed, half-wrecked by thinking *you might leave.*

It winds up with an ecstatically agonized refrain—he doesn't just repeat the words, he puts the same spin of tone and melisma on them every time: "And if you leave me/If you leave me/There's only one thing I can do now/There's only one thing I can say/There's only one thing I can do now/There's only one thing I can say/There's only one thing I can say . . . "

By now he's fully desperate, bracing himself and us for an explosion. But starting the song by crowing "I lost someone" would make it sound exultant, and instead he slips down a key and lowers his voice nearly to a murmur, clipping off his words and purring like Nat "King" Cole. The girls in the crowd do his screaming for him as soon as he hits the first two words. He can't keep it to himself for long, though, and after seven words of his bottled-up sensitive act, he's howling again. For the rest of the verse, his two natures fight word-by-word for territory—he rips open "heart" and tears at it for a few seconds, then spins the end of it into a genteel lead-in for the buttoned-up "bleed."

As soon as the second verse starts and the horns blurt in like peeping toms falling through a trap door, JB casts off the Mr. Collected routine and starts pleading rawly. If he hasn't actually fallen to his knees by this point, he might as well have.

THE KNEES OF JAMES BROWN

James Brown does not, as a matter of routine, perform without begging, repeatedly. Not being one for half measures, he does not beg without falling to his knees. He falls to his knees half a dozen or so times in every show: on soft wooden floors like the Apollo's, on hard concrete stages, on carpet, on stone, on metal, on earth. Four or five shows a day, three hundred days a year, in the early years. A hundred or more shows a year, even now that he's in his seventies. Fifty years in show business. Imagine James Brown falling to his knees for his audience tens of thousands of times, probably hundreds of thousands of times. Imagine the scar tissue, inches thick, on the knees of James Brown.

LOST SOMEONE

It sounds like he's flicking away the verse structure at this point, but he's not—it's actually a relatively faithful reading of the song, which was a couple of verses followed by loose vamps on its original 1961 recording. The effect, though, is of a lover with a fraying tether clinging to a few phrases: "I love you tomorrow," "help me," "I'm so weak." When he repeats "I love you tomorrow" four times, he casts it differently every time. You can hear the torn flesh at the back of his throat. One of those times, he seems to be calling for a snare-drum accent, to no response. "But oh yeah. Oh yeah. But AAAAAAAAH-huh." This time he gets his snare hit.

HOW HARD IS JAMES BROWN SINGING?

There's a bootleg audience recording of James Brown playing at the University of Virginia fieldhouse in Charlottesville on March 12, 1965. It's muffled and spotty; the horn section is barely audible; the microphone is distorting. But you can hear JB loud and clear. He starts the 45-minute set with "Out of Sight," singing nice and tough—anybody else's version of floor-walking R&B shouting. Halfway through "Prisoner of Love," though, something comes over him, and he starts *screaming* so hard that the microphone is quaking under his voice. For most of the next half-hour, he's howling, possessed, spraying blood. Even the crooned parts of "Lost Someone" sound like they've been dragged over miles of gravel. Listening to it, you realize: when he recorded LATA, he knew he was being recorded, and he held *back*, so he wouldn't overload the microphone and get distortion all over the recording, because then Syd Nathan would never let him put it out. *Live at the Apollo*, my friends—*Live at the Apollo* is the sound of James Brown *holding back*.

LOST SOMEONE

James Brown psyches himself up with a few more warmup phrases—maybe rising to his feet again?—and eases his voice into the cadences of gospel quartet singing.

GREAT MUSICIANS KEEP THEIR EARS OPEN

So is the sanctified-sounding "Lost Someone" based on a particular great gospel song? Nothing of the kind: both Brown and Bobby Byrd, who co-wrote it, have noted that they based it on the one-step-forward-two-steps-back chord changes from country singer Conway Twitty's 1958 No. 1 hit "It's Only Make Believe." The resemblance isn't close, but it's not absent, either. Brown and company recorded the relatively controlled studio version of "Lost Someone" on February 9, 1961. Released that November, it hit No. 2 R&B, No. 48 pop.

LOST SOMEONE

"Sometime I get a little trouble," James Brown announces twice, "but let me hear you say yeah." One woman in the crowd responds with a holler, but most of them are too mesmerized to realize they're supposed to scream back. He calls for a "yeah" again, a few more times, with increasing vehemence, and this time they notice. "I love you tomorrow. I LOVE." By this point, we've shifted back into the realm of the deeply secular. This time, he's not begging any more; he's in control. "I want you to come on," he sings (stepping away from the microphone—far enough away that most singers would be lost, but he is less quiet than anyone else who's ever tried to croon). The "on" almost drops off; it's superfluous; he just wants her to come.

And then he starts to go on about "I need your love so bad now," and he's falling into one of his standard traps. James Brown, as fully self-possessed as he is, has rarely been able to be *fully* James Brown when he could be one of the singers he admires for a moment instead; here, he's quoting Little Willie John's "Need Your Love So Bad" in words and tone. (After John was killed in prison a few years later, Brown recorded a tribute to him, *Thinking About Little Willie John and a Few Nice Things*.)

It's reasonable that JB was remembering Little Willie John at that particular moment, though. James Brown and the Famous Flames' first appearance at the Apollo had been in the spring of 1959, promoting "Try Me"— Little Willie John was the headliner, and the bill also included the Upsetters (who had backed up both Brown and Little Richard), Butterbeans & Susie (an old-school vaudeville comedy duo who'd been kicking around for a few decades, and later toured with the Brown revue), and Vi Kemp, a little-remembered R&B singer and contortionist.

Underscoring JB's performance throughout "Lost Someone" are some fine, understated organ parts, reportedly played by Bobby Byrd of the Famous Flames, rather than Fats Gonder. Byrd has never had anywhere near the glory, grace or ego of James Brown, but a few longtime observers swear that he was the heart of the Brown operation.

BYRD

The Flames were originally Bobby Byrd's band, which had evolved in 1953 from a group known variously as the Gospel Starlighters and (for their secular performances) the Avons. James Brown, who'd been released from Georgia Juvenile Training Institute into the care of Byrd's family, was their drummer, at first. (There's an early photo of him behind the kit, smiling as if he knows he'll seize power before they know what's hit them.) When they recorded "Please, Please, Please," Byrd had expected it to be released under the Flames name, not "James Brown and the Famous Flames."

So it was, though, and so the name stayed. Byrd remained Brown's right-hand man through the early '70s (that's his voice doing the call-and-response with JB on "Sex Machine" and "Soul Power"), and reunited with him occasionally as late as 2001. Between 1963 and 1973, he released 25 Brown-produced singles, 7 of which made the R&B charts. But, as he told interviewer Cliff White, "with James running things, you could never get a hit as big as his." Even when Brown was producing and promoting Byrd, there was occasionally a subtle element of humiliation to it, of reminding him who was boss. The title track of Byrd's only JB-produced album was "I Need Help (I Can't Do It Alone)." It was his biggest solo hit, recorded in mid-1970 over a year-and-a-half-old backing track for a discarded version of the song that later became Brown's smash "Mother Popcorn." The writing credit on "I Need Help" is "Teddy Brown"—who was James's teenage son.

LOST SOMEONE

James Brown stays a little ways off from the microphone for a spell, plotting out his next move, maybe working the crowd, shaking and slapping the hands extended to him from the front rows, repeating the gambits he pulled out a minute or two earlier. (People in the crowd are yelling things, trying to get his attention.) Then he comes back and sighs straight into the mic: "Help me, somebody . . . I love you tomorrow . . . "

His face is turned up toward the microphone. He's a short little guy, but he always positions the mic above his mouth (not below or directly in front of it, as most singers do). It opens up his throat, and gives him a look of prayerful imploring.

MICROPHONES

Among his many gifts, James Brown is a master of microphone technique. The publicity photographs of the other members of his revue are of them looking elegant and vivacious, usually with a mic nowhere in sight. The classic photographs of Brown almost always involve a mic: pulling it toward his open and screaming mouth, dipping it like a dance partner, pushing it to the side as he turns away in psychic torment. His mic stand is specially weighted so that it can bounce right back to a standing position when he bends it over, then whirls away from it.

LOST SOMEONE

The LP version of LATA ends its first side by fading out in the middle of "Lost Someone," right around here (during the "I'm so weak" bit), and then fades right back in as Side 2 begins. This was an unheard-of trick for a pop album at the time—the only kind of vocal music that was long or tricky enough to get the fade-out/fade-in treatment was opera.

You can't see James Brown's hands on the record, but you can tell this is when he made his move. (There are videotapes of him moving a single hand behind his back, like a karate chop, to cue a sudden stop.) The band cuts, sharply, on the first beat. The silence hangs in the air like a missile.

SILENCE

On October 24, 1962, at (for the sake of argument) let's say exactly the same time, John Cage, in Tokyo, wrote a piece called "0'00" (4'33" No. 2)," which was "to be performed in any way by anyone." It was dedicated to Toshi Ichiyanagi and Yoko Ono.

FRIEDRICH NIETZSCHE ON THE SUBJECT OF JAMES BROWN, MORE OR LESS, FROM *THE BIRTH OF TRAGEDY*

"The Dionysian musician lacks any image and is in himself only and entirely the original pain and original reverberation of that image . . . He can say 'I' because he is the moving central point of that world. Only this 'I' is not the same as the 'I' of the awake, empirically real man, but the single 'I' of true and eternal being in general, the 'I' resting on the foundation of things."

LOST SOMEONE

"I!" James Brown announces—not the Southern "ah" he's been using through most of the song, but a bright Northern first-person imperative. When he slides back into the croon for the start of the next verse, he drops back down an octave. It's abruptly apparent that he's been pleading at the top of his range, and sighing resignation to himself at the bottom. Incidentally, the single version of "Lost Someone," edited from the Apollo performance, starts with that high "I" at 5:05: an explosion, not an insinuation.

"I lost someone/a million to one/ten thousand people/under my father's son/who need someone . . ." Meaning is slipping away from him, but literal meaning is no longer the point. Bass player Hubert Perry gets totally lost at the end of the verse, and Les Buie follows him into lostville as they enter the next section of the song, but somebody in the audience is feeling it—she screams just as they hit that first note, loud and hard, and the crowd around her bursts into laughter and sympathetic screams. James, preaching, is guardedly sympathetic with his band while he's working the sexual frenzy of the crowd: "You know we all make mistakes sometimes/And the only way we can correct our mistakes/ We got to try one more time." Perry and Buie play no more clams for the rest of the song.

But James is pushing all the right buttons. "I wanna hear you scream. I wanna hear you say OW!" Which they do, of course, but not enough: "Don't just say ow, say OW!"—and in a brilliant conversion of the sacred to the utterly secular, he follows that by purring "And I believe my work will be done." Now down to business: "OW!"

Is he still pleading? There's a weird bit about not going to his next-door neighbor instead of him—but he switches gears into all-knowing preacher again: "I believe somebody over here lost someone." To which a woman shoots back: "Yeah, you, baby, you! Ha-ha-ha . . . yeah, you!"

"It's getting a little cold outside," he declares, and there's a rustling of assent. (It was: the weather on the night of October 24 was nasty, in the mid-to-upper 30s Fahrenheit in Harlem. Brown's staff had gone out and handed complimentary cups of coffee to people waiting in the long line outside the Apollo, making sure they were in a good mood when they got inside.) But then he adds: "I wonder do you know what I'm talkin' about? I said it's gettin' a little *cold* outside." That's a nudge. He's not talking about the weather. He's talking about the chill everyone in the room has been feeling for the last two days. But that's outside; this is inside the temple of Apollo, where the famous flames burn.

"You know, I like to sing this song," he sings, and somebody ripostes: "Go on, sing your song"—twice. "It make me think about the good things"—what, is he going to go back into "Think"? But he's got one particular good thing in mind. "Ow!" three more times, and then a hum he holds for way longer than you'd think, culminating in a spat "Shucks!"

WHY JAMES BROWN SAYS "SHUCKS"

Another thing that happened on October 24, 1962, was that Lenny Bruce was arrested for a performance the previous night at the Troubador Theatre in Hollywood, where he'd said "where is that dwarf motherfucker?"

LOST SOMEONE

"I feel all right," he declares again—his whole show is flashing before us, time feeding back in on itself. He is more alive than he has ever been. He has everything and everyone to lose. "I feel so good I wanna SCREAM."

A DIGRESSION: 1992

James Brown is performing at Madison Square Garden's Paramount Theater, singing "It's A Man's Man's Man's World," the song that took the protracted-ballad place of "Lost Someone" in his show in the mid-'60s and has stayed there ever since. "I feel just like I wanna

SCREAM," he declares. "I just wanna SCREAM. Is it all right if I SCREAM?"

The woman a few seats away from me is in her fifties: well-dressed, well-manicured, came in wearing a nice hat, possibly saw JB thirty years earlier, now totally losing it, yelling back at the stage: "SCREAM baby— SCREAM baby—"

A DIGRESSION: 1962

Nobody seems to have reviewed the October Apollo engagement, but *Variety* did write about the Brown revue's Apollo bill on May 30, 1962: "His act includes clowning, vibrant hoofing, emotional singing and even the tossing of such various items to the crowd as his bow tie and cuff links. Latter gesture triggered a bit of fisticuffs between a couple of femmes in the audience over the tie."

LOST SOMEONE

"I feel just like I wanna scream, but"—and the scream cuts off the "but" as it flies out of him— "AAAAAAAAAAhaaaaa!" The stick connects with the snare, the knees collide with the ground, the scream goes curling up from the microphone and around the note. James Brown has been singing "Lost Someone" for almost *eleven minutes*. Time has bent and suspended under the week's incredible gravity. Pop songs, in 1962, are two and a half minutes long, or three, or (freed from the confines of a 78 RPM record) perhaps four, or if they're split into two parts maybe even six—not eleven. One more melismatic run, one more little shout, a hand gesture, a showman springing to his feet, and the band freezes, and so does time—

THE DEATH OF SPONTANEITY

The star of the show has been riding the flow of the audience—"Lost Someone" occasionally touches base with its origins as a song, but it's really a vamp and an unscripted eruption. But Mr. Please Please wants nothing more than to please his audience, so they'll keep coming back. When LATA came out, "Lost Someone" was its centerpiece; the song that kept going for exactly ten minutes and forty-three seconds on the radio was given an immutable form, and took over from the song that kept going as long as it had to go on stage. Two years after it came out, the biggest hit of James Brown's career wasn't any of the middling singles he'd put out in 1964: it was still *Live At The Apollo*, and that meant "Lost Someone," played as close to verbatim as he could justify. The March 1965 Charlottesville show captured on that bootleg mentioned earlier has "Lost

Someone" at its core: eleven minutes of it, starting with a slightly tweaked version of the catalogue of hits, and continuing through the same ad-libs, the same "don't just say ow say OW" routine, the same buildup to the scream, the same arrangement. It's just sung much, much harder. He's had lots of practice.

By the 1967 shows that became *Live at the Apollo, Vol. II*, he'd had a string of hits bigger than the initial LATA; he'd also worked up a new open-ended slow one, "It's A Man's Man's Man's World," which he could riff on *ad lib*, and still does 35 years later. But a few minutes into the Apollo II version of "Man's World," he abruptly slips in a couple of minutes of "Lost Someone" anyway.

PLEASE, PLEASE, PLEASE

Having stretched out to give "Lost Someone" room, time contracts again, this time pushing eight songs into 6 1/2 minutes. It doesn't *seem* like a medley, exactly—it just seems like one hit after another.

It's an abrupt shift in tone: Brown has been crooning and preaching, and all of a sudden he's barking and begging. "Please, Please, Please" is the original hit and central song of James Brown's career—he hasn't actually performed it at every show he's ever done, although you wouldn't be too wrong if you thought so. And the problem with icons like "Please, Please, Please" is that they accrue stories around them. It's not clear exactly how it got written; it appears to have been developed as a variation on the Orioles' 1952 red-vinyl hit "Baby Please Don't Go" (itself a variation of a much older blues song), sometime around early 1954. In *The Godfather of Soul*, Brown acknowledges that the Flames (as the group was then called—no "Famous" yet) used to cover the Orioles song, but suggests that it inspired him to compose "Please, Please, Please" in its own right. Not to contradict the guy who would know best, but listening to "Baby Please Don't Go," it's easy to picture what *might* have happened: The Flames sang "Baby Please Don't Go" one night and let the groove go on for a while; James extemporized by just singing "please! please! please! please!" over and over for a whole verse; the women in front went wild; the Flames decided that the parts of the song that didn't foreground the "please" were just so much baggage, dumped them, and ended up with a new song that would keep the ladies screaming.

The Famous Flames made a demo recording of "Please, Please, Please" in late 1955; talent scout Ralph Bass heard it on the radio and signed them to a contract with King Records. He recorded them playing it on February 4, 1956, with a band including Fats Gonder on piano. King's owner Syd Nathan, in what was either one of his legendary bad decisions arising from grouchy moods or an apocryphal example of same, claimed to hate it; according to Bass, Nathan said that "to prove what a piece of shit it was, he'd put it out nationwide." (Yes, of course, people spend money to put out records because they hate them, all the time.)

Released on King's subsidiary label Federal, "Please, Please, Please" eventually got all the way up to No. 5 on the R&B chart, remained on the chart for 19 weeks, and kept selling even after it fell off. (In 1960, it bubbled up at No. 105 on the pop chart.) It's one of the simplest songs ever to become a standard: one chorus with small variations, over and over. It's also dirty as hell. Check out that middle verse, as James Brown sings it: "I just wanna hear you say I, I, I, I, I, I, I, I, I, honey please don't go . . . " He just wants to hear her say what? What's the original lyric he's playing with here? There is none—he just wants to hear her make inarticulate rhythmic noises. Fair enough. "Every chick I played it for went crazy," Ralph Bass said, by way of explaining why he pressed Nathan to release it.

The song is actually so minimal that all James Brown has to do is sort of gesture at it, and it happens. Which is what he does for the twenty-five seconds that kick off the medley on *Live at the Apollo*. "Please plea plea plea," he spits, and then he's off the mic and dancing, or collapsing, or something—all you hear is the band, the Flames faithfully doing their backup singing parts, and the frenzied girls, some of whom are very shrill. One of them is shrieking in rhythm before he's even asked her to.

FROM HAL NEELY'S LINER NOTES ON THE BACK COVER

"This is a full package of pure delight."

JAMES BROWN, ALLEGEDLY QUOTED IN THE AFOREMENTIONED AND KIND OF DUBIOUS ARTICLE FROM THE JANUARY 1961 ISSUE OF *SEPIA* MAGAZINE CALLED "THE AMAZING POWER OF JAMES BROWN," ON THE SUBJECT OF A "FINE, YOUNG, SWINGING CHICK" WHO ALLEGEDLY JUMPED OFF THE BALCONY OF THE ROCKLAND PALACE IN NYC DURING ONE OF THEIR SHOWS

"We were giving everything we had with 'Please, Please, Please,' and suddenly this chick became hysterical. It seemed as though our music and singing had set her soul on fire. The Flames and I saw her body sweep away like she was going up in smoke, and the next thing we knew she had swept and swooned herself to the balcony . . . and leaped over. We didn't dig that action at all, but I guess the Flames music just set her on fire, that is . . . musically speaking. Of course we're glad she pulled through."

A PHOTO CAPTION FROM THAT SAME ARTICLE

"Feet wide apart, arm high over head, Brown goes into song with abandon as do most top rock and roll singers, but he packs so much feeling into his music that, like his audience, he is almost overcome with emotion."

OPERATIVE WORDS THAT ARE TOO EASILY FORGOTTEN

"Rock and roll singers."

YOU'VE GOT THE POWER

Three footstomps and we're into "You've Got the Power," originally a duet with Bea Ford (the first woman singer to tour with the Revue, and Joe Tex's ex-wife). Brown recorded it February 20, 1960, released it as the flip side of "Think," and ended up with an unexpected extra hit (R&B No. 14, pop No. 86). The writing credit was split between Brown and original Famous Flame Johnny Terry; he wasn't singing with the group any more at that time, but he was doing promotional work for the revue.

"You've Got the Power," at least the ten-second-long nod to it on LATA, starts abruptly—"But ohh-uh, I need you darlin' . . . " That's the way the original single starts, too, smack in the middle of a verse. It's not the way the song as written, or as originally played, starts: Ford got an opening verse that went "I'm leaving you darling/And I won't be back/I found something better/Somewhere down the track," which makes the rest make a little more sense. Apparently, someone decided that it was a bad idea for a James Brown single to have its first lines sung by somebody other than the star, so the song was lopped off to the point where JB started singing, and performed that way ever after, even when Brown re-recorded it with Vicki Anderson in 1967.

Perhaps Yvonne Fair sang it as a duet with Brown some nights. It's not unlikely that she wouldn't have been in the mood to sing it with him that particular night.

I FOUND SOMEONE

You might think this was an answer song to "Lost Someone"—it's not, but it might as well be, and it's been retitled that way for the sake of LATA. Brown first recorded the song as "I Know It's True" on November 11, 1959, and released it under that title on his *Think!* album the next year, as well as on the B-side of "I'll Go Crazy." It's notable for having the worst drumming on any issued James Brown recording—Nat Kendrick can't make up his mind whether he wants to play straight sixteenth notes on his hi-hat or swing them, and the result is just a mess.

On LATA, James Brown only gives us 39 seconds of it, but we're not missing much of the song's substance. One of the trumpet players botches another couple of notes. Even so, the band's on much firmer ground than they are on the studio recording, and Brown sings it like an actor working through line readings: "*I* found someone—to love me. I found *someone* to love me . . . " And Fats Gonder is on the case—check out the way he underscores JB's most vehement "*loooooove*" with a swell of organ, swiping a finger down the keyboard once the singer lets go.

MEANWHILE

At around this time—1 in the morning, let's say— Johnny Prokov, a bartender at the National Press Club, told Anatoly Gorsky of the Russian news service TASS that he'd overheard a conversation between two journalists a bit earlier that night, to the effect that the invasion of Cuba was supposed to start the next day. Within hours, the information was relayed to Premier Khrushchev.

WHY DO YOU DO ME

James and three of the Famous Flames split the writing credit for the four songs recorded at their first session: "Please, Please, Please" went to Brown and the very lucky Johnny Terry, as did their second single, "I Don't Know." The B-side of the former, "Why Do You Do Me," was credited to Bobby Byrd and Sylvester Keels (as was a later B-side, "I Won't Plead No More," which is functionally identical to "Please, Please, Please"); the remaining Flame, Nashpendle Knox, split the credits on "I Don't Know"'s B-side with guitarist Nafloyd Scott. All four songs were recorded on February 4, 1956; "Why Do You Do Me" later turned up on Brown's second album, *Try Me!*, in 1959.

Beginning on the beat after "I Found Someone," "Why Do You Do Me" sounds like a continuation of it—maybe even the second half of a verse. Again, there's only a four-line fragment of it in the medley, a mere 25 seconds or so. But Brown doesn't quite sing it like himself: he drops his voice down to polite crooning territory as the horns swing in lockstep.

I WANT YOU SO BAD

Another 25 seconds, another four lines, another anony-mous 6/8 ballad. "I Want You So Bad" had originally been the inauspicious follow-up to "Try Me," recorded December 18, 1958, in the middle of a West Coast tour, and released the following February. Brown sang it with almost exactly the same inflections as "Try Me," but he didn't have nearly as notable a song to work with, and it stalled at No. 20 on the R&B charts, ap-pearing there for only two weeks as "Try Me" finally fell off after almost half a year.

So the choice of a title for the cash-in album that contained both singles, released late in 1959, was obvi-ous: the aforementioned *Try Me!* The original album cover features a painting of an attractive black woman with an impossibly tiny waist, holding a cigarette, from which smoke is not rising, and a gun, from which it is; none of the band are pictured. (The front cover also lists the song "Messing With the Blues" as "Messing With the Birds.") In 1964, once LATA had established Brown's album-artist credentials, King reissued *Try Me!* as *The Unbeatable 16 Hits*, with a cover featuring photo-graphs of Brown on the ace, king, queen, jack and ten of hearts. "I Want You So Bad" is listed on both covers as "(You Made Me Love You) I Want You So Bad."

The song made one more bizarre appearance in the Brown discography: in late 1964, with Brown off recording for the company's competitor, Smash Records, King shoved out the seven-year-old "Fine Old Foxy Self" as a single, and made its B-side the "I Found Someone"/"Why Do You Do Me"/"I Want You So Bad" part of the Apollo medley, re-edited to nudge it over the two-minute mark.

It was around this time that another plane armed with nuclear bombs took off from Westover Air Force Base in the direction of Russia. They were taking off every hour, just in case.

I LOVE YOU, YES I DO

Originally a No. 1 R&B hit for Bull Moose Jackson and His Buffalo Bearcats in 1947, "I Love You, Yes I Do" carried a writing credit for Henry Glover and Sally Nix. Glover was an arranger for Lucky Millinder, and probably the guy who actually wrote the song; "Sally Nix" was a pseudonym for none other than Syd Nathan, who released it on King and raked in multiple kinds of royalties. Jackson—whose first name is sometimes spelled as Bullmoose—had a recorded persona that was half softie and half world-class horndog (he's also the guy who recorded the deliciously smutty "Big Ten Inch Record," for instance). His version is rather square: clarinets, enunciation, operatic breath control. Jackson re-recorded "I Love You . . ." in 1961, and had an R&B success with it again (No. 10), even clawing at the bottom of the pop charts. James Brown had recorded a cover of it with his band in February of that year, and it appeared as a single once Jackson's new version started to become a hit in September; while Brown didn't chart with it, the B-side, "Just You and Me, Darling," went No. 17 R&B.

We get a full minute and a half of it on LATA—having sung five song fragments in a row at the same pace, Brown finally shifts gears here. (Note that he sets the tempo by singing the first few words by himself.) He's in full-on crooner mode, the band is simmering rather than boiling, and the audience is audible again. Including the "little old lady": right after the line "from the way I look at you," at 2:36, she yells "sing it, [something garbled], sing it!" (It's probably not "motherfucker.") At 2:52, a scratchy, male voice announces "sing a song, James." Could it be covering something else up there?

Turning up "I Love You Yes I Do" as loud as it can go is also a good way to admire the amazing recording quality of *Live at the Apollo*. You can make out the cries in the crowd, and bits of the Famous Flames' off-mic backing vocals; you can also hear a little squeak right before each beat. Perhaps the drum kit had a squeaky hi-hat, or the organ had a squeaky speaker?

In any case, "I Love You . . . " ends *very* abruptly, certainly more abruptly than the band is expecting (they spend a few seconds scrambling to find their place). The lyric Brown is about to sing is "you set my world on fire," to complete the rhyme, but what he actually sings is "you set my world—but I wanna let you know one thing/I wanna tell you one thing/I wanna tell you one thing/As I was walkin' down the street, yeah—" It's not inconceivable that something was cut from this point in the medley, too—something feels strange about the pause, and the key-change, and the grammar of "I want to tell you one thing: as I was walking down the street, why does everything happen to me?" doesn't make much sense, not that that's ever stopped James Brown before.

Even so, the band's failure to stop perfectly on a dime indicates something amazing about the LATA performance. The medley is not switching between songs according to a preset arrangement, it's being played *as Brown cues it*. Go back and observe: every song in the medley begins with Brown singing its first few notes before the band comes in. The only exceptions are "Why Does Everything Happen to Me," which gets the little fanfare we've just heard, and "You've Got the Power," where he has a few seconds of footstomping to mouth the title to his band. In fact, he cues "Lost Someone" and "Night Train," too, and you can hear Clayton Fillyau's ka-thump as the boss brings his hand down to cut off every song. When you play with James Brown, you have to watch his hands at every moment.

WHY DOES EVERYTHING HAPPEN TO ME

James Brown is a rhythm and blues singer, not a blues singer—he recorded very few straight-up blues numbers, but the rasping force of these two choruses suggests that he might have had another calling, as well. James and the Flames initially recorded "Why Does Everything Happen To Me" at their fourth King session, on April 10, 1957. They had undoubtedly picked it up from Roy Hawkins' hit from seven years earlier. As with most postwar R&B hits, there's quite a story behind it; as usual, it involves lots of people taking credit for it.

Bob Geddins, who likes to call himself the "God-father of Oakland blues," was an Oakland, California record producer and owner of half a dozen tiny labels. As the tale runs, Geddins wrote a song called "Why Do Everything Happen To Me" for singer/pianist Roy Hawkins, who'd had an arm paralyzed in a car accident, and sold his rights to the song to Jules Bihari, who ran Modern Records with his brothers Saul and Joe. Bihari, under his songwriting pseudonym "Jules Taub," split the official writing credit with Hawkins, and it went on to become a No. 2 R&B hit on Modern in February

1950. (To add to the confusion, some pressings of Hawkins' version are labeled as "Why Do Things Happen To Me"—the legal title, according to BMI.)

But take this story with a rock of salt. Bihari had a habit of claiming partial songwriting credits for contributions like being present when the tape machine was turned on; "Jules Taub" is, for instance, credited with co-writing some early B.B. King singles he can't have had much to do with. And as for Geddins' story of being inspired by Hawkins' accident to write a song for him but beneficently not take credit for it—well, Geddins didn't exactly have a lot of hits on his own.

On top of all this, the composer credit on some versions of James Brown's recording reads "James Brown." Well, he corrected the grammar, which might be more than Bihari or Hawkins did. Brown's version didn't turn up on record until 1959, when it was an album track on *Try Me!*—listed as "Strange Things Happen"—and it reappeared as the B-side of "Night Train" in early 1962, this time as "Why Does Everything Happen To Me." Between the time when Brown recorded it and released it, though, B.B. King released his own version of "Why Do Everything Happen To Me," in 1958; on the Apollo recording, Les Buie is constantly playing licks that sound a lot more like King's than like his own. (Once again, Brown loved his peers a little too much—even on stage in the early '70s, he'd yell "B.B., c'mon!" to his guitarists to let them know he wanted that specific kind of blues solo.)

BEWILDERED

James Brown has performed "Bewildered" more than almost any other song, and there is a chance he may not actually know how its melody was originally meant to go.

There are only about 25 seconds of "Bewildered" on LATA, but it's got one of the twistiest histories of anything James Brown performed that night. Teddy Powell and Leonard Whitcup wrote it in 1936; the first hit recording was trombonist Tommy Dorsey's extraordinarily square version of 1938. (Mildred Bailey recorded it that year, as well.) Listening to Dorsey's recording after years of hearing Brown's is a shock: the chord sequence is the same, but it has a completely different melody, far more the sort of thing you'd expect to hear from Tin Pan Alley in the mid-'30s than the extravagant, blue-note-laden melisma Brown throws at it.

So how did it get from one form to the other? The answer probably lies in 1948, when everybody started recording "Bewildered." In December of that year and in January 1949, the Red Miller Trio and Amos Milburn's respective versions of "Bewildered" fought it out for the No. 1 position on the R&B chart. Both re-cordings, especially Milburn's, slow "Bewildered" way down and play up the heavy, rolling triplet feel of the song; both versions have a distinctly different melody from both the Powell/Whitcup original and Brown's later cover (although they're a little closer to each other). And Milburn's version adds a vaguely sleazy saxophone answering every phrase of the verses. Brown mentions hearing both versions in his autobiography, although the text, put together by Bruce Tucker, calls Miller "Red Mildred."

In response to the hits, other artists jumped onto the "Bewildered" bandwagon. Billy Eckstine and the Quartones' recording with Hugo Winterhalter hit R&B No. 4 and pop No. 27 in early 1949; even the Ink Spots took a crack at it that January. Brown's first band, the Cremona Trio, sang it too. After that, it dropped off the pop-culture radar for a decade, and resurfaced in a minor hit cover for Mickey & Sylvia in June 1958 (No. 57 pop)—this time without the triplets, with yet another melody (more or less derived from Miller's version), and with slightly altered lyrics.

Mickey and Sylvia's "Bewildered" had no audible influence on James Brown's version, which he recorded not long after, on January 30, 1959 (he'd made a demo a few months earlier). But he'd clearly been thinking about the song for a few years. Back at their third professional recording session, on July 24, 1956, James and the Famous Flames recorded an original song called "Just Won't Do Right," whose chords are basically identical to those of "Bewildered." (He was very fond of "Just Won't Do Right," and recorded it a few more times under various titles over the next 15 years—as 1970's "Since You Been Gone," it's a speedy, one-chord-plus-bridge funk vamp.)

As fine a performance as it was, Brown's "Bewildered" ended up sitting unissued for almost two years, until it finally showed up on the *Think!* album at the end of 1960. He kept singing it live anyway; released as a single at last in February 1961, it went to No. 8 R&B and No. 40 pop.

The 1959 Brown "Bewildered" owes more to Milburn's version than to any other. (Years later, Brown nodded to Milburn again, splitting the single version of Fred Wesley & the J.B.'s' 1974 "Damn Right I Am Somebody" into "part 1" and "last part that went over the fence," a line from Milburn's hit "Chicken Shack Boogie.") But the melody is a deep-soul improvisation on Milburn's melody, which itself is an improvisation on the original. JB pushes it almost ridiculously hard—the opening "bewildered" gets sung on ten notes, shifting the emphasis to the third syllable, leaping up like a shocked man for the little burst on the mid-word "d" and then spiraling morosely on its way down.

(At his peak, Brown could fine-tune the amount of soul spin he'd put on any song. For a great example, see his 1966 single with two versions of "The Christmas Song," accompanied by the same backing track: one a relatively straightforward Ray Charles/Charles Brown–style reading, the other a wild workout.)

Oddly, having come up with this daring and seemingly effortless melodic variation-on-a-variation, Brown has sung "Bewildered" exactly the same way ever since. And that's how he sings the four lines of it on LATA: tracing its curlicues precisely, without particular regard for the lyric, except as a prop for a sequence of wails he's executed thousands of times before.

PLEASE, PLEASE, PLEASE

The central piece of schtick in James Brown's career is his "Please, Please, Please" cape routine. He drops to his knees, overcome with emotion, sometimes feigning a heart attack. One of his henchmen rushes over, drapes a cape (originally a coat, or a towel, or a robe) over him, and leads him away, patting his back gently to the beat of the song. Suddenly, at the end of a chorus, James Brown stamps his feet, tosses off the cape, whirls around, strides back to the microphone and sings another chorus. Then he collapses again. This happens a few times. Finally, he's led offstage. He was already notorious for it by the time of LATA; the publicity photo in the Apollo's ad that week is of someone helping the agonized Brown to his feet.

He's been doing it near the end of almost every show for over 40 years, and it still works every time—it makes for great theater. But the recorded evidence isn't quite as compelling. *Pure Dynamite!*, the live album he recorded in 1963, includes an unabridged live "Please, Please, Please," meaning there are painfully long stretches with the band vamping, the Flames flaming, the crowd screaming and nothing happening under the spotlight. If that's what was happening at the Apollo, it was probably a good idea to cut it down drastically for the album.

(*Pure Dynamite!*, released in February 1964 by King Records, with whom Brown was then having some contractual difficulties, was meant to capitalize on the success of the unstoppable LATA, which was still on the charts after almost a year. It is recommended to every musician considering making a live album as an example of what *not* to do—it fails in nearly every way that LATA succeeds. The sound quality of the recording, from Baltimore's Royal Theater, is catastrophic; two tracks are obviously studio recordings with crowd noise dumped over the top. Its absurdity reaches its limit when the instrumental vamp at the end of "Signed, Sealed and Delivered" gets an MC *describing* the dance James Brown is doing: "Oh, he's on one leg now. He's changed to the other leg! . . . ")

Clearly, a live version of "Please, Please, Please" had some commercial potential—the original single kept selling for years, and both the song and the idea of a live recording were synonymous in the public eye with James Brown. But the split-up minute-and-a-half on LATA clearly wouldn't do, either, and neither would the murky, half-Brownless version on *Pure Dynamite!* It was evident that, although Brown sang "Please, Please, Please" hundreds of times every year, he would probably never again sing it straight. King punted; at around the same time as *Pure Dynamite!*, they re-released the original 1956 studio recording of "Please, Please, Please," with added crowd noise. And the ruse worked, at least a little, getting to No. 95 on *Billboard*'s Hot 100 on February 15, 1964 (there wasn't an R&B chart at that time).

The last minute of the Apollo medley is a pair of unusually straight choruses of "Please, Please, Please," which is to say that the rudiments of the lyrics are not entirely replaced by strangulated yelps (although we do get a couple of them, gloriously enough). He even re-peats his trick from the original recording of singing one chorus not quite as hard, like a lover murmuring sugary things, before he shrieks the final line.

What matters here, though, is the *image* that "Please, Please, Please" calls to mind, of James Brown enacting the agony of near-death and a sudden resurrection fueled by desire, tying up the sexual-abandonment narrative of the album. The Apollo's audience would have made that association even if he didn't actually do it on stage—if the image of the suffering man being helped to his feet weren't already iconic, it would be a very weird choice of photo to put in an ad.

NIGHT TRAIN

This one's got a peculiar and convoluted history. The train-horn-style descending blues riff at the core of "Night Train" was first recorded in Chicago, on November 2, 1940—it showed up in the second chorus of the Duke Ellington Orchestra's "That's the Blues, Old Man," credited to saxophonist Johnny Hodges.

The Ellington Orchestra recorded their "Deep South Suite" on November 23, 1946, in New York. Its fourth section, "Happy Go Lucky Local" (credited to Ellington and Billy Strayhorn), is a galumphing six-minute stomp, originally split over two sides of a 78 RPM disc, that goes into some wild territory in the middle. But it opens with a piano playing what would later become the B-section of "Night Train," and the last couple of minutes of the song return to that theme. (Ellington re-recorded "Happy Go Lucky Local" in 1960 for his *Piano in the Background* album, in a sprightlier, shorter version.)

Sonny and Charlie Harris adapted **Ellington**'s piece as "Happy Go Lucky Local Blues," **and** the vocal group the Orioles recorded it on March 20, 1951. On September 6 of that year, they played at the **Apollo**, along with the Johnny Hodges Orchestra. Maybe **the** two riffs first met that night. They would definitely become acquainted by the end of the year.

Tenor saxophonist Jimmy Forrest played with Ellington in 1949 and 1950. In the early '50s, he struck out on his own and started an R&B band. At a November 27, 1951, recording session in Chicago, he put the Hodges riff next to the Ellington/Strayhorn riff, slowed it down to stripper-on-the-bar-top speed, added a walking blues bassline (played by Johnny Mixon), gave the whole thing a nice hard grind, called it "Night Train," and signed his name to the composer credit.

Or, rather, it was almost his name—the original single credited him as "Jimmy Forest"—and he got part of the composer credit. "Night Train" was released as an instrumental on the Chicago label United, run by an entrepreneur by the name of Lewis Simpkins. Lyricists get a chunk of money when songs they've co-written are recorded or performed—even as instrumentals—so Simpkins wrote a set of fairly awful words to Forrest's instrumental. In his version, the Hodges riff starts "Night train/That took my baby far away," and the Ellington riff starts "My mother said I'd lose her/If I ever did abuse her/Shoulda listened." (The mysterious Oscar Washington got co-writing credit too.) Q-Tip, of the hip-hop group A Tribe Called Quest, put it best on "Check the Rhime," half a century later: "Industry rule number four thousand and eighty/Record company people are sha-dy."

In any case, Forrest's "Night Train" was an enormous smash, a No. 1 R&B hit for seven weeks in 1952. (When James Brown was released from incarceration on June 14, 1952, it might have been playing on the radio.) But it didn't show up at all on the pop chart: black audiences bought it, white audiences didn't. So trombonist Buddy Morrow (born Muni Zudekoff) promptly covered it with his band, in a slightly speedier version that nonetheless has a lot less life in it—the Mixon bass line is replaced by nearly inaudible piano, and a Morrow trombone solo in the middle bogs it down badly. Even so, Morrow's version was a No. 27 pop hit; he subsequently billed himself as "The 'Night Train' Man."

"Night Train" became something of an R&B standard. Wynonie Harris took a crack at a vocal version in the summer of 1952. Rusty Bryant sped it up to double-time, called it "All Night Long," and released it as a single in 1955; for a while, it was disc jockey Alan Freed's theme song on his influential show on New York's WINS. Bill Doggett recorded "Night Train" for King Records in 1959, with his usual rock-steady groove, speeding it up even further and playing the bass part on the organ—by this point, it was a song you could dance to in front of a jukebox, without even taking your clothes off. In July 1960, "Night Train" was a minor pop hit (No. 82) for the Viscounts; harmonica player Richard Hayman also got a No. 82 out of it in September 1961. Sandy Nelson made the charts with a drum-centered version of "All Night Long" in July 1962.

James Brown recorded his own version of "Night Train" at the knockout session of February 9, 1961, that also produced "Lost Someone" and "Shout and Shimmy." He displaced drummer Nat Kendrick from the kit, and played drums and sang at the same time (his fills are enthusiastic, if a little shaky). Brown's version is mostly a showcase for J.C. Davis's tenor sax, dispensing with the triplet swing of earlier "Night Train"s in favor of a brisk, straight-ahead bam-bam-bam-bam. He also dispenses with Simpkins's words, if indeed he ever heard them in the first place, in favor of hollering a list of cities—a gimmick to ingratiate himself with local DJs. (James Brown was into list-of-cities songs at the time:

"Mashed Potatoes U.S.A.," a more-or-less improvised lyric sung over the instrumental "Limbo Jimbo," announces his intention to do the mashed potatoes in every city he could call to mind, ending with a misspelling of his home town—"that's A-G-U-S-T-A." It was a No. 21 R&B hit, and Brown's latest single when he played the Apollo.)

CITIES

On October 24, 1962, John F. Kennedy, in a meeting with his cabinet, asked if there was any way that the U.S. could evacuate its major cities before an invasion of Cuba. Somebody at the table assured him that "the only real protection" from nuclear bombs was cities.

NIGHT TRAIN

"Night Train" turned up late in 1961 on an album, *James Brown Presents His Band and Five Other Great Artists*, but wasn't released as a single until March 1962, and finally became a hit: No. 5 R&B, No. 35 pop. Thirteen years later, the J.B.'s recorded a discofied instrumental variation on the Hodges riff, "All Aboard the Soul Funky Train"; this time, the composer credit was simply "James Brown."

At the Brown revue's shows in the fall of 1962, "Night Train" was the standard finale. There's a photograph of Brown, his jacket cast off and his shirt and cummerbund sagging, soaked through with sweat, followed by the Famous Flames (you can tell because they have white tailored shirts with "Famous Flames" embroidered on them), the 5 Brownies in their shimmery metallic dresses, and finally poor Yvonne Fair, wearing a much chaster textured dress. They're all in a sort of conga line, dancing on the lip of the stage to "Night Train" at the end of a show. James Brown is executing some kind of complicated knees-and-arms move, lips curled back a little as he concentrates on his footwork; his eyes are cast down and to his left, at the front rows of the audience. "Baby Lloyd" Stallworth is directly behind him, eyes focused intently on the boss. The Brownies have spotted the photographer, and are flashing grins at him. Yvonne, all the way at the back, is smiling wanly at the dancing girls, her feet tight together.

Brown's shouted introduction on *Live at the Apollo* is a good excuse to switch keys, even with what sounds like the "little old lady" yelling "NIGHT TRAIN!!" too early a couple of times. It's also the conclusion of the album's narrative, and the final echo of Fats Gonder's introduction: "I said I lost someone"—bam bam, just like the beginning of "Lost Someone"—"but I know where I'm gonna find them"—bam bam—"all aboard"—yeah, shouts the band—"all aboard"—yeah, shouts the band—"all aboard the night train!" It is not, after all, the end of the world; there is always another place to go, another city, and there's always another girl, always another girl.

What follows is about as fast as it's possible to play "Night Train," especially at the end of the fourth two-hour gig of the day. The "That's the Blues, Old Man" riff is intact; the "Happy-Go-Lucky Local" riff is reduced to a series of breathless blurts. But the core of this version is the bass line Mixon devised, doubled on guitar and accompanied by thunderous drumming. (The rhythm section's take on it here took on a bit of its own life: former gospel singer Bunker Hill's 1963 single "The Girl Can't Dance" is an obliteratingly fierce Little Richard-style screamer, accompanied by Link Wray's Raymen playing the Apollo "Night Train" groove even faster.)

The cities Brown lists are something like an East Coast tour itinerary, and they were also hot spots for black radio—the stations he hoped would play LATA. Washington, D.C., was the site of the Howard Theater, where they'd be November 16–25; Baltimore had the Royal Theater, where they'd be November 2–11; Philadelphia had the Uptown Theater, where they'd been August 24–September 2, as well as an "American Band-

stand" broadcast back in June where he'd sung "Night
Train" and "Shout and Shimmy." "All aboard for New
York City" is a sop thrown to the audience in front of
him; Boston is where he'd be four days later, at the
Arena. As for "I believe there's some places I didn't
go"—well, he may be the only one who believes it.

After the 2:30 mark or so, Brown's no longer singing,
aside from an almost inaudible holler around 2:48—he
and the other singers are conga-lining off the stage.
He's never been one to bother with the "thank you very
much, good night," curtain-calls or encores, he just
dances off when he's done with his last song for the
night, whether everyone else is done or not. Once he's
safely backstage and the curtains are being drawn, Lewis
Hamlin cues another abrupt stop.

I MAY BE WRONG

But there's one more tune fragment—if you've got most
versions of *Live at the Apollo*. The other "mystery song"
on LATA didn't appear on the earliest pressings of the
album, which faded out by the end of "Night Train."
"I May Be Wrong (But I Think You're Wonderful)" is
a standard by Henry Sullivan and Harry Ruskin, introduced by the roly-poly ("perfect 46") vaudeville comedi-
enne Trixie Friganza and Jimmy Savo in a 1929 revue
called "John Murray Anderson's Almanac." Popularized

among black audiences by John Kirby's 1939 recording, it was also the Apollo's own theme song, played at the beginning or end of every show (or both), by either the house band or whatever band was featured that week. By this point, the theater's great curtain had closed: time for everyone to go home, back to the terrifying world.

TIME, DEFORMED

"I May Be Wrong" is the oldest song the band played that night, but not by much—in the space of a single set, they'd touched on music from the '20s, '30s, '40s, '50s and '60s. The medley alone is a mini-tour of 20th-century black popular music up to that point: blues, ballads, R&B, Southern soul, transfigured Tin Pan Alley, all refracted multiple times through interpretation, mutation and theft. But it doesn't *feel* like a survey of history. All of that past and all of those singers are subsumed into a single overwhelming voice, whose nostalgia for the songs he heard on the radio as a kid has exactly the same tone and force as his nostalgia for a tune he came up with by himself a couple of months ago. (He's been known to confuse the two categories.)

But time also collapses forward from the moment of the Apollo show. James Brown invented funk—and hit his artistic stride—a bit over two years later, with "Papa's Got a Brand New Bag." He's had over 100

R&B hits since October 1962. Brown the R&B shouter is, in some ways, only a footnote to the career of the guy who recorded "Cold Sweat" and "Say It Loud—I'm Black and I'm Proud" and "Make It Funky"; *Live at the Apollo* is not the work of that guy, except inasmuch as its stripping away of song form cleared the way for records built from rhythm. There are thousands of records that bear James Brown's influence, and a lot of them even namedrop him, but almost all of them take off from his 1965–1974 funk period. You can scarcely hear the echoes of the massively popular *Apollo* in the music of anyone other than James Brown himself.

It's possible to extrapolate forward from the formal elements of LATA to the formal elements of the funk years: the hyperextended vamp of "Lost Someone" prefigures the endless grooves of the early-'70s hits; the buildup to the scream anticipates the buildup to the bridge; the "Hold It" link suggests the sour, choppy guitar playing all over Brown's great dance singles. Consider *Apollo* for a moment, though, from the perspective of the people in the room where it was recorded, living in the biggest target in the world at the single most threatening, uncertain moment they'd ever known— Dean Rusk called it "as grave a crisis as mankind has ever been in"—with war machines flying overhead. That performance, James Brown's all-out bid for the glare of stardom, his invention of himself-as-art, must have felt like the climax of all of history. The rhythmic explosion wouldn't take place for another few years, but something was happening, and everybody could feel it. We can hear them scream as they feel it. Or can we?

THE MISSING SCREAMS

Weirdly enough, the audience is much quieter on "Night Train" than on the rest of the album, even when JB offers his shout-out to New York. At the end of the show, when you'd expect them to be cheering their heads off, they're all but silent. Chuck Seitz, the chief engineer at King Records, mastered *Live at the Apollo*. He tells the story: "The tapes came down from New York, and they had very, very little audience on them. I suggested we try to boost the audience up. I went out to Roselawn, to a sock dance they used to have out there. I knew the DJ, so I went out there with a tape recorder. He got them to applaud and cheer, and I went back and inserted it where it was needed." And the "little old lady"—did Seitz have instructions to try to remove her interjections? "Oh, we left that in there," he says, chuckling.

An educated guess: *Live at the Apollo* was mixed backstage with a pair of headphones, as it was happening. There were eight microphones, and a couple of them were aimed at the audience, but they fed a 2-track Ampex machine. Whoever recorded it (the album credits Tom Nola as "location engineer," but Hal Neely reports that he recorded it himself) must have turned the audience mikes down when the crowd was expected to cheer, so it wouldn't overwhelm the rest of the recording, and up to catch mid-song interjections and whoops. The screaming crowd you hear on *Live at the Apollo* wasn't there at all. The screaming crowd at the Apollo, the audience whose full-throated catharsis fuels James Brown's performance, can barely be heard. Smoke and mirrors, special effects.

DON'T TELL A LIE ON ME AND I WON'T TELL THE TRUTH ON YOU

There's one other small fiction about *Live at the Apollo*, in which this book has participated. By all accounts, it wasn't entirely "the actual recording of the midnight show," as Hal Neely's sleeve notes claimed—Brown's team taped multiple performances (all that night), and assembled the best ones. (And, although there was an 11:00 show that night, the Apollo only had a midnight show on Saturday.) But the fiction is such a fine one, and so close to the truth. Oh, and the bear thing? Might've been the next night.

BACKSTAGE

What happened after the show? There's some dispute. Hal Neely claims that "James hadn't seen his mother in twenty years, and she showed up backstage at the Apollo that night." Brown's autobiography says that that particular reunion happened three and a half years earlier—the first time he played the Apollo, opening for Little Willie John in April 1959.

One person we do know was there was Cassie Stokes, who'd been hired that week as Brown's personal bodyguard. A little puff piece that ran in the December 1 *Pittsburgh Courier* noted that she was "a judo expert who quickly ejects undesirables attempting to crash the star's dressing room"; she stayed with the revue for four years.

THE NEXT NIGHT

Let's assume that Brown and the band stuck around for the wrap party on Thursday night at the Palm Cafe (they were due to play in Wilmington, Delaware, on Friday—a four-hour drive at worst). They'd have broken bread with Hank Ballard and the Midnighters. Ballard was, arguably, one of the models for Brown's career. His group had first broken onto the charts in 1953, under the name the Royals (until the "5" Royales made them change their name), and they'd had 20 hits since then, including "Work With Me Annie" and the original version of "The Twist." The Flames' general presentation was inspired by the Midnighters', and a lot of the early James Brown singles (like "Begging, Begging") were attempts to imitate Ballard's groove.

A short piece in the new issue of *New York Amsterdam News* began: "Hard on the heels of James Brown and his revue, the Apollo announces the appearances of Hank Ballard and the Midnighters and another exciting revue—the one in constant rivalry with James Brown." In truth, though, there wasn't that much competition left between them: Ballard had made his final appearance on the pop charts with "Do You Know How To Twist" back in February, and hadn't been seen on the R&B charts since the previous August's "Nothing But Good." Within the year, Brown would be producing the first two in a string of more than a dozen singles for Ballard, including his only remaining R&B hits— and those wouldn't come out until 1968 and 1972. And Brown demanded a terrible kind of obeisance from everyone he helped, and from his old hero Ballard more than most.

FLASH FORWARD TO 1972

Hank Ballard, audibly slurring his words, is extemporizing into a microphone to the instrumental track of

James's overwrought hit "World." Or maybe he's taking some cues off a script. It's hard to tell:

I'm Hank Ballard, the "Love Side" man. Rapping for you on the contents of James Brown's latest album . . . yeah. A living legend. That's what they call him, a living legend, and guess what, that's what the man is: a real, live, living legend. Yeah, after 18 years, he's still terrorizing the music world with his funky music. [Could he be sneering a little?] And judging from his new album, he's still on the good foot of his career. James Brown world. James Brown world of music. Oh well, he deserves to be in the galaxy of stars. But it wasn't easy for James from the beginning. He had to fight his way through a mean, vicious jungle, you know, the jungle of show business. It's vicious, I tell you, I mean, very vicious, actually, I know. And my advice to all newcomers is that if you're timid and looking for mercy stay on the road that leads to a more compassionate world. 'Cause this one I know will eat you up alive, brother. I mean, alive. Yeah, I got caught running around the graveyard of losers. [A sigh.] But I had an unshakeable determination that I was coming out: this is not my place, you know. So I came out and joined the James Brown production. [By this point he sounds like he's trying to ward off tears, and not the kind that come from gratitude.] James was the only one besides myself that had a strong belief in my talent. I knew he could formulate a groove that would put my style back into this galaxy, you know. [Rousing himself:] James Brown world, James Brown world of music! And wow, I'm glad I'm part of this world.

This is not a fan-circulated bootleg; it was hung out for everyone to hear. It was released on Brown's 1972 album *Get On the Good Foot* as "Recitation by Hank Ballard."

YVONNE AND TAMMY

And Yvonne Fair? What about her? Yvonne had to go home. Yvonne, as it turns out, was pregnant with James's son. She left the tour after the band's engagement at the Apollo. But there's always another girl, always another girl. "I tended to go with whoever was my lead female singer on the show at the time," Brown brags in his autobiography. "So, on the road, she'd be with me."

(A year later, Henry Stone's Florida label Dade put out another JB-produced single by Fair, "Straighten Up"; one final new single, a cover of Bobby Byrd's "Baby Baby Baby," squeaked out in 1966. By then, she'd been touring with Chuck Jackson for a year. She turned up again in the '70s, this time at Motown, where she made an album called *The Bitch is Black*.)

Buddy Nolan, one of JB's road managers, came from Philadelphia—he used to manage a club called the Tan Playhouse there. When the James Brown revue played at Philly's Uptown Theater the week of August 24, he introduced the star to a 17-year-old girl named Tammy (Thomasina) Montgomery. By the time the tour hit Baltimore at the beginning of November, Tammy had taken over Yvonne's solo spot, and the boss had his eye on her too. (Four months later, she was recording "I Cried," a song Brown and Byrd wrote with the chords that would later become "It's A Man's Man's Man's World." Released on the Try Me label, it poked its head in at No. 99 on the pop charts. Five months after that, she left the revue. A couple of years after that, she was Motown star Tammi Terrell. A few years after that, she was dead.)

SOMETHING FOR NOTHING

The November 3 issue of the black paper the *Pittsburgh Courier* ran a little article on James Brown's Apollo shows—an undigested press release, really:

> NEW YORK CITY—You would think they were giving away something for nothing at the Apollo The-atre (*sic*) last week. The lines were that long and the people were that enthusiastic though unbelievable to the unconverted. The attraction was James Brown the sensational delineator with his big show and big band [. . .] a show which the Apollo management said is all entertainment to all theatregoers.

THE ALBUM

But the hype had an element of truth to it. The recording was great—everybody agreed on that from the
first. Even Syd Nathan, who'd originally dismissed the
idea, loved the result. "One thing that was pleasant to
me was that Syd got excited about *Live at the Apollo*,"
Chuck Seitz reports. "He didn't get excited about anything." He agreed to buy the tape, and released *Live at
the Apollo* the following spring, as King LP 826, although
his expectations for it were still astonishingly low.

Harry Weinger, a Polydor Records archivist and
James Brown expert, has dug up King's original pressing
order: 5000 copies of the LP and 8000 copies of the
sleeve—not many, particularly considering that King's
pressing and printing plant were both housed within the
company's facility in a converted icehouse in Cincinnati.
But that was standard operating practice for him, according to Seitz: "Syd's theory was that he'd put 1000
copies of a record out, and then watch it real close—he
wouldn't advertise until something started to take off."

Music-industry magazines *Billboard* and *Cashbox* reviewed it with a sort of noncommittal hype; neither
reviewer appeared to have listened too closely. *Billboard*
wrote: "The exciting set was recorded during an actual
performance at the Apollo Theater, and the shouts of
the crowd, the electric of the music bursting on the

audience and their reaction for a dynamic 40 minutes or so." (Yes, there appear to be a few words missing from that sentence as published—and 40 minutes is what the back cover says, not what the album contains.) *Cashbox* noted that "the songster's distinctive, highly-personal style is showcased on a bevy of favorites including . . . 'You've Got The Power'"—a song of which LATA includes roughly ten seconds.

But the world did catch on. *Live at the Apollo* snuck onto the album charts on June 29, and stayed there for 66 weeks (it peaked at No. 2 that summer). There wasn't an R&B album chart yet in those days—LATA's success, in fact, paved the way for the R&B album market—but it certainly would have hit the top if there'd been one. It was requested constantly on radio stations—not its individual songs, but the whole damn thing, which DJs who knew what was good for them played every day, with commercials between halves of "Lost Someone."

Curiously, it took a bit longer for the black press to latch on to Brown. Neither *Jet* nor *Ebony* covered Brown at all in 1963, even as *Live at the Apollo* was selling at a furious clip. Their music sections focused, instead, on more respectable types like Duke Ellington, Aretha Franklin and Little Stevie Wonder. Brown didn't have the image that those magazines valued in their cover stars. He was unclassy through-and-through: crude, loud, flashy, self-important, showoffish about his wealth. He showed very little interest in the civil rights movement, at least in public—that changed abruptly with 1968's "Say It Loud—I'm Black and I'm Proud" and his switch from an immaculate process hairdo to an afro, but legend has it that his consciousness was raised by a grenade left in his dressing room by Black Panthers. ("I'm more than just an artist," Brown declared in a 1968 Apollo performance telecast that June as *James Brown: Man to Man.* "I want you to know that I'm a man—a black man—a soul brother." It was as if he *had* to say it.)

How many copies did *Live at the Apollo* end up selling? Who knows? Syd Nathan probably knew, and he wasn't telling—he apparently didn't bother to get RIAA certification for King records. (A number of King acts have complained about sales accounting that was, to put it mildly, vague.) It stayed in print through the '60s, and has been intermittently in and out of print since then, from various labels; Polydor's 1990 budget-line edition was replaced, in 2004, by a "deluxe" version with four single edits appended to the original album.

BACK TO THE APOLLO

Just over a year after Brown's *Apollo*, Atco Records recorded a bunch of their stars for the *Apollo Saturday Night* album: Otis Redding, Rufus Thomas, Ben E. King and more. Within a few years, there were "Live at the Apollo" albums by half a dozen other artists. But they were all trying to trade on the cachet of the original. The venue was half a pop star now, and the star had a little bit of venue in him. Playing live at the Apollo was what James Brown did; James Brown was the guy who did *Live at the Apollo*. He came back to the theater every six months or so for a decade, even when he could have been playing much bigger venues.

The November 11, 1964, issue of *Variety* includes a full-page ad for James Brown and his revue, centered on a sycophantic letter from the Apollo's Robert Schiffman ("My dad and I want you and all show business to know how happy we are over the record-breaking business which the JAMES BROWN REVUE did here last week"). The bottom of the ad reproduces the covers of Brown's latest album, *Showtime*, as well as *Live at the Apollo*. And the lineup of the revue is almost entirely Brown's band and protégés: The Famous Flames, Bobby Byrd, Elsie "T.V. Mama" Mae, the Five Royales, Anna King, guitarist James Crawford, Pigmeat and Comedy Co., Danny Ray, and Al "Brisco" Clark (the saxophonist from the Apollo band, who got a single credited to him, "Soul Food," in June 1964). Clark wasn't much longer for the revue at that point, but he'd learned his lesson from the Apollo gig—he appears as the emcee on an early 1966 recording of Otis Redding's live show (released years later as *Good To Me*), and his introduction owes rather a lot to Fats Gonder's LATA opener.

James Brown's own *"Live" at the Apollo Volume II* was recorded June 24 and 25, 1967 (before the first night, he was given a plaque to mark one million tickets sold to his Apollo shows—almost certainly an exaggeration), and released a year later; it went to No. 2 on the R&B charts, and No. 38 on the pop charts. The third Apollo live album was *Revolution of the Mind*, recorded in July 1971, with the inexperienced but energetic band who'd just replaced the classic lineup with Bootsy and Catfish Collins, and released five months later: No. 7 R&B, No. 39 pop.

He kept coming, but the expectations for his Apollo shows eventually got too high. His "Black Caesar Show" at the Apollo in May 1973 was picketed by activists who wanted him to do a benefit for community groups; John Rockwell, in the *New York Times*, called the show "poorly paced yet too obviously calculated." After that, Brown stopped playing at the Apollo quite so often; the venues got big, the new records got small. The next time he made an album there, it was *Live at the Apollo 1995*, actually recorded in September 1994, and about which the less said the better.

AND NOW

And now? Yvonne Fair is gone. So are "Fats" Gonder and Hubert Perry, and "Baby Lloyd" Stallworth, and Lewis Hamlin Jr., and Dicky Wells, and tenor saxophonist St. Clair Pinckney (hear James calling on his late-'60s singles: "St. Clair!"), and Freddie King, and Pigmeat Markham. And so are James's manager Ben Bart, and Buddy Nolan, and Gene Redd. For every person who was in the audience at the late show on October 24, 1962, there are fifty who remember it perfectly.

James Brown is still recording and touring, still falling to his knees. He returns to the Apollo every year or two; in November 2003, he played a pair of shows there to mark the 40th anniversary of the original *Live at the Apollo* (or, well, the 41st or so).

JAMES BROWN, INTERVIEWED FOR AN EARLY-'90s PUBLIC TELEVISION DOCUMENTARY, ON THE SUBJECT OF THE APOLLO THEATER

"The Apollo Theater is like blood in the veins of the people . . . Humanity should own the Apollo. God should own the Apollo."